THE GREAT
BOOK OF
NEW YORK

The Crazy History of New York with
Amazing Random Facts & Trivia

**A Trivia Nerds Guide
to the History of the
United States Vol.2**

BILL O'NEILL

DON'T FORGET YOUR FREE BOOKS

GET THEM FOR FREE ON
WWW.TRIVIABILL.COM

CONTENTS

CHAPTER TWO

CHAPTER THREE
FACTS ABOUT NEW YORK CITY'S ATTRACTIONS

CHAPTER FOUR
NEW YORK INVENTIONS, IDEAS, AND
MORE! 87

CHAPTER FIVE
NEW YORK'S UNSOLVED MYSTERIES,
SUPERNATURAL, AND OTHER WEIRD
FACTS 109

CHAPTER SIX
NEW YORK SPORTS: BASEBALL,
FOOTBALL, AND MORE!

INTRODUCTION

How much do you know about the state of New York?

Sure, you know New York City is a tourist hotspot. You know it's home to the New York Yankees, the New York Giants, and Broadway. But what else do you *really* know about the city?

You know the Statue of Liberty was a gift from France, but do you know which popular New York City attraction sees more annual visitors than the Statue of Liberty?

Have you ever wondered how New York came to be known as the Empire State? Do you know why people call New York City the "

'Big Apple'? Have you ever wondered if it actually has anything to do with apples?

Do you know which war New York state played a key role in or which President was sworn into office in New York?

If you have ever wondered the answers to any of these questions, then you've come to the right place. This book is filled with stories and facts about the state of New York.

This isn't just any book about New York. It will highlight some of the key facts that have helped shape New York into the state it is today. You'll learn facts about the state that you've probably never even wondered about. Once you've finished reading, you'll know all there is to know about New York.

New York is a state that's rich in both history and culture. We'll go back in time before New York City was what it is today. We'll jump around and look at some of the coolest (and most shocking) elements of the state's history and explore some of the more recent happenings of the state.

Although, we'll mostly stick to a timeline of historical events, we'll also jump around some as we talk about some of New York's past and some of the most famous people who live in the state.

This book is broken up into easy to follow chapters that will help you learn more about the Empire State. Once you've finished each chapter, you can test your knowledge with trivia questions.

Some of the facts you'll read about are sad. Some of them will give you goosebumps. Some of them are shocking. But the one thing they all have in common is that all of them are fascinating! Once you've finished reading this book, you're guaranteed to walk away with a wealth of facts you didn't know before.

This book will answer the following questions:

Why is New York City called 'The Big Apple'?

How did the state of New York come to be known as the Empire State?

Which iconic late comedian is honored by a festival that's held in her hometown every year in New York?

Which BBQ restaurant in the Big Apple is owned by a former '90s boy band member?

What famous lake monster is believed to live in one of New York's lakes?

Which famous athletes were born in New York?

And so much more!

CHAPTER ONE

NEW YORK'S HISTORY AND RANDOM FACTS

New York City Got Its Name from the Duke of York

It's hard to imagine New York City being called anything else today, but did you know NYC was once called something else? The city's former name was New Amsterdam.

An early Dutch settler named Peter Minuit purchased what is now the present-day island of Manhattan from the Native Americans in the early 1620s. The reason he bought it was to legitimize Dutch claims to the territory. Minuit is said to have paid the Lenape tribe in $24 worth of trinkets or jewelry. It's been estimated that he paid the equivalent of about $1,000. Minuit named the island New Amsterdam, of which he became the first governor of.

In 1664, the territory of New Amsterdam was seized

from the Dutch settlers by the British. During that time, King Charles II changed the territory's name. He named it after his brother the Duke of York, who was responsible for organizing the mission.

New York Was a Key Battlefield During the Revolutionary War

Did you know New York played a critical role in the Revolutionary War? Due to its central location in the American colonies, the state was at the forefront of the war, especially early on.

Opposition from New York residents also played a big role in the war. The people of the state were opposed to the Stamp Act in 1765, which required everyone to pay a tax on paper products such as newspapers, licenses, and playing cards. Many became resistant to the act.

A secret society called the Sons of Liberty was formed to protest the Stamp Act. While it was formed in Boston, there was a large New York branch.

Some of the most significant battles of the Revolutionary War took place in New York. In fact, one of the first battles of the war took place in 1775 when Ethan Allen and Colonel Benedict Arnold captured Fort Ticonderoga. The cannons that were captured at Fort Ticonderoga were dragged to Boston and used to help stop the British attack that was happening there at the time.

On August 27th, 1776, the Battle of Long Island occurred. The battle was the largest of the entire Revolutionary War. The British won the battle against George Washington and his troops, leading the British to gain control over Manhattan.

At that time, Washington withdrew from the battles. Many of his supporters viewed his withdrawal as a smart tactic because it caught the British army off guard.

After Washington had left Manhattan in British hands, many New Yorkers fled. As they fled, however, many American prisoners were also brought to the city. In fact, at one time, Manhattan was housing 30,000 American prisoners, many of which were being kept there under horrible conditions. Many of the Continental soldiers were also held as prisoners on British ships in the New York Harbor, where they were also treated under awful conditions.

The Battle of Saratoga was another one of the most important battles of the Revolutionary War. Led by Horatio Gates and Benedict Arnold, the battle is considered the turning point of the war. It's the battle that convinced France to enter the war as America's ally. The battle also gave Americans renewed hope for winning the war.

After the Revolutionary War was won, the last British troops left Manhattan on November 25th, 1783, which would later come to be known as Evacuation Day. The day was celebrated throughout the country into the 1800s.

New York City Was the First Capital of the United States

Today, it's hard to imagine the nation's capital being located anywhere other than Washington D.C.. You probably know that Philadelphia was the country's capital at one point, but did you know that New York City was actually the very first capital of the United States?

New York City became the first capital in the United States in January of 1785. The old City Hall on Wall Street is where the Congress of Confederation convened at that time. The old City Hall building was later remodeled so that it could become the United States' capitol building. At that time, Congress met and held their meetings at Fraunces Tavern.

At one point, lower Manhattan was going to become a federal district. The presidential mansion was to be built on Governor's Island. However, keeping NYC as the nation's capital was very controversial. Some feared that the city was too aristocratic and leaned towards England's styles of clothing too much.

Needless to say, New York City's time spent as the country's capital was short-lived. It only lasted for five years, between 1785 and 1789. The last time Congress convened in New York City's Federal Hall was on August 12th, 1789.

George Washington was sworn into office as the first President of the United States at Federal Hall on April 30th, 1789. This is why a statue of Washington can be located outside of a reconstruction of Federal Hall can be found today!

New York Was Probably Nicknamed the "Empire State" by a United States President

New York is known as the 'Empire State', but no one actually knows for sure how the state got its nickname. That being said, there are a number of theories.

A lot of people very wrongly assume the state was nicknamed after the Empire State Building. In reality, the state's nickname came first.

It has been theorized that the state was nicknamed the 'Empire State' because of its variety of resources, such as its fertile soil, rich timberland, and its abundance of water. This may be at least part of the reason New York got its nickname. Even in early history, the state's growth and prosperity likely had to do with the reason it got its nickname.

It's believed that George Washington may have been responsible with nicknaming New York the Empire State. The first time the state was referred to by its nickname in documents was in 1784. During that time, George Washington said his vision for the state was as "the seat of the empire." He believed New York's central location and its abundance of resources would make it a significant unifying state for the rest of America.

No matter how New York got its name, it's quite fitting. The state is somewhat of an empire with both national and global significance.

The nickname was used on New York license plates from 1951 until the mid-1960s and again from 2001 until now.

The Fight for Women's Rights Started In New York

Did you know that the fight for women's rights kicked off in the state of New York? In July of 1848, the first *ever* convention for women's rights in America took place in Seneca Falls, New York. It was held at the Wesleyan Chapel.

Nearly 200 women attended the convention, which was started by two abolitionists named Lucretia Mott and Elizabeth Cady Stanton. The convention was attended by famous African-American abolitionist Frederick Douglass.

Two weeks after the convention, there was an even larger one held in Rochester, New York. After that, women's rights conventions were held every year.

In 1917, women won the right to vote in New York. By 1920, the 19th Amendment had been adopted, which gave all American women the constitutional right to vote.

The Five Boroughs of New York City Used to Be Cities of Their Own

Modern-day New York City is known for its famous five boroughs: Manhattan, Queens, Brooklyn, the Bronx, and Staten Island. But did you know that there once was a time when the five boroughs were cities entirely of their own?

In fact, it wasn't until 1895 that people in Queens, Brooklyn, the Bronx, and Staten Island voted to consolidate with Manhattan in order to form 'Greater New York.'

Brooklyn almost didn't become part of New York City. There was an anti-consolidation movement in the city. It voted in favor of consolidating with Manhattan but only by 278 votes.

The consolidation had a huge effect on the size of New York City. In December of 1897, New York City's size was 60 square miles and its population was just over 2 million. When the five boroughs officially consolidated on January 1st, 1898, NYC's size grew to 360 square miles – or six times its previous size – and its population increased to more than 3.35 million people.

Why is New York City Called the 'Big Apple'?

Have you ever wondered how New York City came to be known as the 'Big Apple'? For a long time, no one really knew where the nickname came from. People speculated and came up with many theories.

Some people figure the city got its nickname because New York State is the second top state in the country for apple production and has a lot of apple orchards. This isn't the reason, however.

Another popular theory was that there was a brothel-operator named Eve in New York City and that the name originated from Adam, Eve, and the forbidden apple. This theory was eventually to put to rest as nothing more than a rumor.

So, what's the real reason New York City came to be known as the Big Apple? The nickname actually stems from horse racing.

The big horse racing tracks throughout New York City were referred to as 'apples.' It's believed that the nickname was given to the tracks because horses liked apples.

A reporter named John J. Fitz Gerald was the first one to mention the "Big Apple" when he described it in *The New York Morning Telegraph* around 1920 as going to the "big time." Fitz Gerald allegedly heard African-American stable workers in New Orleans say they were going to "the Big Apple," since NYC was known for its big-time horse racing venues.

Fitz Gerald continued to call New York City the Big Apple in his newspaper columns. The nickname caught on in the 1930s when jazz singers began to use the term regarding NYC's big-time music clubs. In 1950, Frank Sinatra used the name when describing the city in an NBC radio program. The rest is history!

Ellis Island Was Used for Pirate Hangings in the 1700s

Ellis Island was one of the main immigration stations in the United States. More than 12 million immigrants passed through the station. It has been estimated that four out of 10 Americans can trace at least one of their ancestors to Ellis Island. But before it became a federal immigration station in 1892 and for sixty years after, Ellis Island had a past that might surprise you.

Ellis Island was once used as a hanging site for convicted pirates. Mutinous sailors and other criminals were also executed there. During the 1760s, the island became known as 'Gibbet Island' due to the gibbet—or wooden post—where the dead bodies were displayed after they were hung.

The last hanging took place on Ellis Island in 1839.

After that, the island's name was reverted back to 'Ellis Island,' which it had been given after Samuel Ellis, who owned the island.

The island, which was leased from Ellis by the State of New York in 1794, later went on to become a military post. It served as a military post for almost 80 years before it was eventually chosen to be a federal immigration station.

The first immigrants who passed through Ellis Island in 1892 were unaccompanied minors. They were 17-year-old Annie Moore and her two younger brothers, who had immigrated from Ireland to meet their family in New York. Annie Moore was given a $10 reward for being the first immigrant to pass through the station. Today, a statue of the siblings can be found at the Ellis Island Immigration Station.

In1954, Ellis Island saw its last immigrant come through the station, a Norwegian merchant named Arne Peterssen.

The island, which opened to the public in 1976 and then again in 1990, now gets about 3 million visitors a year!

There Was a Holocaust Refugee Shelter in Oswego, NY

A little-known fact of American history is that President Franklin D. Roosevelt saved the lives of 982 war refugees during WWII. They were brought to Safe Haven, a refugee shelter located in Oswego, New York.

In 1944, President Franklin D. Roosevelt sent his Special Assistant to Italy to carefully select which refugees to bring back to the United States. The first priority was given to refugees who had managed to escape from concentration camps, but people who had skills that would benefit the camp were also chosen.

The refugees technically had no legal right to be in the United States. President Roosevelt promised Congress that the refugees would later return home to their original countries once the war was over.

The refugees traveled aboard the USS Henry Gibbons. The trip is said to have been an awful one, with the refugees suffering from seasickness, cramped quarters, and overheating during the two-week journey. When they arrived at the New York Harbor, they were excited to be greeted by the Statue of Liberty.

When the refugees got to Safe Haven, however, they didn't feel entirely free. Despite being provided with food, healthcare, and shelter, they still felt imprisoned by the barbed wire fences that surrounded the camp and by the military personnel who guarded them.

There were some silver linings of being at the shelter.

Children went to school. One pair of refugees got married. The people of Oswego were friendly and helped sneak food into the camp.

Despite Roosevelt's promise to Congress, many of the refugees never went home and instead were provided with clearance to remain in the United States.

The Safe Haven Holocaust Refugee Shelter Museum serves as a memorial to the war refugees who lived there. It preserves the history of the only war refugee shelter in the United States.

New York's Hospitals Helped Shape the Healthcare Industry of Today

Today, New York is known for some of the best hospitals in the country. According to a 2013 *US News & World* report, New York-Presbyterian Hospital of Columbia and Cornell ranked as the seventh best hospital in the United States.

But did you know that over the years, New York's hospitals helped shape the healthcare industry today? The state is home to a number of historically significant medical achievements.

The first public hospital in the United States opened in New York in 1902. The Ellis Island Immigrant Hospital was used to house wannabe immigrants who were found to be too unfit to enter the United States. The hospital ran until 1930. It was later abandoned in 1954. The main building became a museum in 1990 and in 2014, the entire hospital could be viewed in hard hat tours. Even today, the hospital is viewed as an extraordinary part of the history of the public health field.

New York is also home to the oldest hospital in America to still be in operation today. Bellevue Hospital in Manhattan was founded in 1736. When the hospital was first founded, it was an almshouse for the poor. In 1787, it became a place of instruction for Columbia University's College of Physicians. In 1861, it was turned into Bellevue Hospital Medical College. It was the first medical college that had connections to a hospital in New York.

Since then, Bellevue Hospital Medical College has made some historical programs and achievements that have helped shape the healthcare industry of today. Some of these include:

- 1869 – The hospital opened the first ambulance service ever. The ambulances were horse-drawn carriages and used a gong to make it through crowded streets.

- 1873 – The first nursing program in the country that incorporated Florence Nightingale's principles opened at the hospital.

- 1874 – The first children's clinic in the United States was opened.

- 1875 – The first emergency room in the form of an emergency pavilion was founded.

- 1879 – The first mental ward was opened at the hospital in the form of a 'pavilion for the insane.'

- 1883 – A residency training program was started at the hospital. The concepts from that program are still used as a model for surgical training today.

- 1884 – Carnegie Laboratory, the first laboratory to study pathology and bacteriology in the country was opened at the hospital.

- 1888 – The first men's nursing school in the country opened at Bellevue.

Bellevue Hospital was home to New York City's first morgue, which opened in 1866.

The hospital also treated more AIDS patients than any hospital in the country. More AIDS patients also died at the hospital than they did at any other hospital in the United States.

America's First and Oldest State Park is in New York

Niagara Falls State Park is a popular tourist attraction today, but did you know that it was the first state park to be developed in the United States?

It took a lot of fighting for the state park to become

what it is today. During the 1800s, early environmentalists were worried about the reduction in the Niagara River's flow. This led to the Free Niagara Movement, in which people believed the land surrounding the Niagara River should be free to the public and should also be preserved from commercialization and exploitation. The most noteworthy person who was a part of this movement was Frederick Law Olmsted, the landscape architect who was responsible for designing Central Park.

It took 15 years of fighting from the Free Niagara crusaders for the state to sign the Niagara Appropriations Bill into law in 1885. This led to the development of the Niagara Reservation. Niagara Falls State Park was designed by Frederick Law Olmsted.

Today, Niagara Falls State Park sees more than 8 million visitors a year. It's home to three waterfalls, which were formed over 12,000 years ago during the last glacial period.

One of the oldest American flags can also be found in the state park. Located at Old Fort Niagara, the flag was captured from the British by the Americans during the War of 1812.

Uncle Sam May Have Originated From New York

Uncle Sam is a popular cartoon that is used to represent the American government. Did you know that the cartoon may have originated from New York?

It has been said that the cartoon was actually a caricature of a man named Samuel Wilson. Wilson, a Troy resident, worked a meat packer. In 1812, Wilson supplied rations for American soldiers during the war. He labeled his meat packages with "U.S.", which stood for the United States. When asked what the 'U.S.' stood for, one of Samuel Wilson's workers jokingly said, "Uncle Sam."

However, there are some historians who doubt the credibility of the story. The earliest reference to 'Uncle Sam' was in 1810. Wilson's meatpacking contract with the government didn't take place until two years later.

NYC Has Some Surprising Former Burial Grounds

Perhaps one of New York City's most chilling secrets is that there are a number of parks, squares, and other locations throughout the city that were once used as burial grounds.

Washington Square Park rests above one of the city's

biggest burial grounds. Between the years of 1797 and 1825, the area was used as a potter's field. Most of the people buried there died due to an outbreak of yellow fever. It has been estimated that more than 20,000 people were buried at the site the park was built on top of. Excavators often dig up bodies. During the 19th century, people claimed to see a blue mist that hung over the park at night due to the remains beneath it.

Madison Square Park was built over an estimated 1,300 corpses. Like Washington Square Park, it was used as a potter's field. Many of the people buried there came from local poorhouses or the nearby Bellevue Hospital. In 1806, the area was turned into an Army arsenal and then later was turned into a parade ground.

Central Park may be one of the city's most bustling places today, but it was built upon a cemetery belonging to All Angels Church. It seems that the bodies were never moved. Over the years, the coffins and graves of people buried in the 1800s have been dug up.

Another spot in the city that was a popular burial ground lays just south of Collect Pond. In the 1690s, African-American slaves and even freedmen were forced to bury their loved ones just outside of the city limits. In 1788, bodies were illegally removed from the burial ground for medical experimentation.

Businesses were later built on the burial ground. It wasn't until the 1990s when bodies were dug up by excavators that the area became marked. A memorial was built in 2007.

Today, New York City buries its unclaimed bodies on Hart Island. The island, which is off the coast of the Bronx, is a burial ground to nearly one million bodies that have been buried there since the late 1860s. Hart Island is not open to the public.

These are just some of the many places throughout the city where bodies were once buried.

New York City is Rich in Titanic History

Whether you're a Titanic history buff or you loved the depiction of the tragedy in the film *Titanic* starring Leonardo DiCaprio and Kate Winslet, you might not know that there are a number of historical landmarks throughout New York City honoring the tragedy.

For starters, you might start by checking out what remains of Pier 54. This is where the Carpathia arrived, carrying the survivors of the Titanic. Although the pier is gone now, the gate can still be seen today.

Down the street, you'll find the Jane Hotel, the hotel where surviving crew members were housed after the tragedy. There is a fountain and memorial for the

Titanic in the front lobby of the hotel, which was restored in 2008.

Titanic Memorial Park is located at the entrance of South Street Seaport in Manhattan. There's a lighthouse monument with a plaque that honors those who were lost in the tragedy.

There's a monument located at Broadway and 106th Street, which honors Isidor and Ida Strauss. Isidor Strauss, who helped Macy's become the world's largest department store, is regarded by many as one of the biggest icons who died on the Titanic. His wife Ida was given the option to leave on one of the lifeboats, but she chose to die with her husband instead.

In Central Park, you'll find a memorial dedicated to William T. Stead. Regarded as one of the ship's heroes, Stead was a British journalist who allegedly helped others get off the ship before dying about it himself.

If you pay a visit to Battery Park, you'll find the Wireless Operators Memorial. One of the names you'll find written on it is Jack Phillips, a wireless operator who stayed in the wireless room seeking out help until he died.

These are just some of the historical sites in New York City that mark the history of the Titanic.

New York City Really is America's Melting Pot

New York City has been called America's melting pot, and for good reason. Estimates have found that one out of every three people who live in New York City was born outside of the United States.

The city is home to some of the highest populations of people from various ethnicities and cultures. As a result, a number of different cultures have influenced the businesses and culture of New York City.

New York City is home to a huge Hispanic population. As of 2010, it was estimated that more than 8 million Hispanics live in the city. Of those, 33% are Puerto Rican, 25% are Dominican, and 13% are Mexican. The Bronx is the borough with the largest Hispanic population, with estimates showing that more than half of its residents have Hispanic roots.

Manhattan's Chinatown boasts the largest Chinese community that can be found outside of Asia. In 2015, it was estimated that there were more than 800,000 Chinese-Americans living in New York City. In Chinatown, you can find everything from Chinese food to Chinese clothing styles. A visit to Chinatown isn't complete without making a stop at the Original Chinatown Ice Cream Factory, which serves Chinese-influenced ice cream flavors, such as almond cookie and peanut butter with toasted sesame seeds.

Chinese New Year is also a huge celebration in Chinatown each year.

As of 2011, it was estimated that there were more than 100,000 Koreans living in New York City, making it the second largest population outside of Korea. Two out of three of those live in Queens. There's also a Koreatown in Manhattan, which is well-known for its Korean restaurants and karaoke clubs. Don's Bogam is a popular Korean BBQ restaurant.

In Astoria, Queens, you'll find the highest number of Greek people outside of Greece. This population has grown since 2010 after the country of Greece experienced a financial crisis. Taverna Kyclades is known as one of the top authentic Greek restaurants.

Brighton Beach in Brooklyn is home to a large Russian community. In 'Little Odessa,' you will find plenty of Russian specialties, including pierogi, borscht, and vodka.

More Jewish people can be found in New York City than anywhere in the world besides Israel. It's been estimated that 1.1 million Jews are living in NYC. This is a huge number when you consider that America's overall Jewish population is around 6.5 million. Borough Park is home to a very large community of Orthodox Jews.

Aside from Warsaw, New York City has the largest

Polish population.

New York City is also the city with the largest Irish population. Due to the potato famine and politics, more people from Ireland lived in NYC in 1850 than they did in Dublin. Things haven't changed much. New York still has more people with Irish ancestry than Dublin.

One area in which you might notice the influence of other cultures in the city? When having a conversation with someone! More languages are spoken in New York City than any other city in the world. The most languages are spoken in Queens, lending it the nickname of 'most linguistically diverse capital of the world.' It has been estimated that about 800 languages are spoken in the Big Apple.

Wondering how so many languages could be spoken in New York City? Dozens of Native American languages, languages from the Mariana Islands, native Mexican languages, Pennsylvania Dutch, and Yiddish are just a few of the *hundreds* of languages that are spoken in the city. It is also believed that at least half of all people living in NYC speak a language other than English at home.

RANDOM FACTS

1. New York City has a huge population. It has the third highest population in America, with only California and Texas having more residents. It has been estimated that one in every 37 people who live in the United States are residents of NYC. There are more than 8 million people who live in the city. More popular live in New York City alone than they do in both Switzerland and Australia combined.

2. Contrary to what you might think, New York City is *not* the capital of the state of New York. The capital of New York is Albany. Founded by Dutch settlers, Albany was originally named Fort Orange.

3. Manhattan's current name came from the Native Americans. Its meaning may surprise you: 'island of many hills.' Although Manhattan did have a lot of hills at the time, most of them have since been flattened in order to make room for urban development.

4. No Walmart can be found in the Big Apple. Since it's the largest corporation in the world, this may come as a surprise to some. It all comes down to

unions. New York is a highly unionized city and Walmart does not allow unions to be formed among its employees. Walmart's attempts to open stores in Brooklyn, Queens and Staten Island have all been unsuccessful.

5. Early Dutch settlers found that there were huge oyster beds in Manhattan. This is why Ellis Island and Liberty Island were originally called Little Oyster Island and Big Oyster Island.

6. Five United States presidents were born in the state of New York. These include Martin Van Buren, Theodore Roosevelt, Franklin Delano Roosevelt, Millard Fillmore, and Donald Trump.

7. Just like every other state, New York has a number of strange laws. It's illegal to wear slippers after 10 p.m., you can be fined $25 for flirting, and farting in an NYC church can get you a misdemeanor. It's also illegal to honk your car horn in New York City (aside from emergency situations), but everyone still does it.

8. A plane crash happened at one point in Park Slope in Brooklyn. In 1960, two commercial planes collided with one another in midair. One of the planes crashed on Staten Island, while the other crashed at the intersection of Sterling Place and Seventh Avenue. Despite the fact that 128 passengers and six people on the ground died in

the accident, there is no memorial. However, the color of the bricks at the top 126 Sterling Place are different in color from the rest of the building due to the crash.

9. The Catskill Mountain House in Palenville, New York was the first grand resort hotel to open in the United States in 1824.

10. New Yorkers love their coffee. It's been estimated that they consume seven times more coffee than other people living in the United States. This should probably come as no surprise, considering NYC is home to more than 1,600 coffee shops.

11. A lot of rich people call New York their home. It has been estimated that one out of every 21 people residing in New York are millionaires.

12. Albert Einstein's eyes can be found in NYC. A doctor who removed Einstein's brain to study it also removed his eyes. The eyes were given to Einstein's eye doctor, who kept them in a safe deposit box in New York City. They still remain there to this day.

13. The Bronx is the only NYC borough which is located on the mainland. The other four boroughs are located on islands. Queens and Brooklyn are both located on Long Island, while Manhattan and Staten Island are both islands of their own.

14. Former first lady and presidential candidate Hillary Clinton's career started out in New York. She served as the first female senator from New York after she was elected in 2000 and was re-elected to office in 2006.

15. The American Museum of Natural History is home to President Theodore Roosevelt's memorial.

16. The oldest cattle ranch in America was not started in the West. It's Deep Hollow Ranch, which is located in Montauk on Long Island. Founded in 1747, the ranch is still open today.

17. The "I love New York" (often represented by a heart symbol in place of "love") was created as a tourism campaign during a countrywide recession to draw more interest in the state. It has been around for more than 30 years and has become a popular slogan both nationally and globally.

18. After the stock market crashed during the Great Depression, a number of New Yorkers committed suicide. It's even been said that one hotel clerk started asking guests if they needed to get a hotel room to jump from the balcony. Some New Yorkers handled the financial crisis differently and began selling apples. In fact, an estimated 6,000 people were selling apples in NYC.

19. In 1992, it became legal for women to go topless in New York City.

20. Apples are the official state fruit of New York. European settlers first brought apple seeds to New York in the 1600s.

Test Yourself – Questions and Answers

1. Which United States President may have nicknamed New York the Empire State?
   a. George Washington
   b. Abraham Lincoln
   c. Bill Clinton

2. Who was the first female senator of the state of New York?
   a. Elizabeth Warren
   b. Condoleezza Rice
   c. Hillary Clinton

3. New York City was the nation's first capital for how many years?
   a. Two years
   b. Five years
   c. One year

4. Which of the five boroughs almost didn't become a part of New York City?
   a. Brooklyn
   b. Queens
   c. The Bronx

5. The Native American meaning of Manhattan is "island of many…"
   a. hills
   b. roads
   c. birds

Answers

1. a.
2. c.
3. b.
4. a.
5. a.

CHAPTER TWO

NEW YORK'S POP CULTURE

Since New York City is one of the biggest tourist attractions in the entire world, it should come as no surprise that the Empire State is rich with pop culture. Do you know which movies and films have been filmed in New York? Do you know which hit TV show that's set in New York City was based on a book? Do you know which movie was based on a true story that happened in New York? Read on to find out the answers to these and other fascinating pop culture facts about the state.

Lucille Ball's Life is Celebrated Every Year in Jamestown, New York

If you're a fan of *I Love Lucy*, then you may already know that Lucille Ball was born in Jamestown, New York. Though her family lived in Michigan, Montana, and New Jersey, Lucille Ball's mom later moved the family back to Celeron, NY, near Jamestown.

Lucille Ball later attended the John Murray Anderson School for the Dramatic Arts in NYC. Her instructors didn't think she would make it in show business, but Lucy was determined to prove them wrong.

Lucy and her real-life husband Desi Arnaz met when they were both cast in the New York production of *Too Many Girls*. The couple later went on to self-produce *I Love Lucy*, which is set in a New York City apartment building.

Today, Lucy's life is celebrated every year in Jamestown. The Lucille Ball Comedy Festival, which is held each August, draws in almost 20,000 people every year from nearly every state!

Each year, there are stand-up comedy performances. Some of the past performers at the event have included Jerry Seinfeld, Ellen DeGeneres, Jay Leno, and more. There are exhibits showcasing Lucille Ball's career. Some of these exhibits have included *Lucy I'm Home* and *The Desi Arnaz Exhibition*. There are Lucy tribute shows with impersonators, a block party, and so many other things for Lucille Ball fans to enjoy!

If you're unable to make it to the festival, that's okay! Jamestown is also home to the Lucille Ball Desi Arnaz Museum, which is open year-round. The museum, which opened in 1996, preserves both the personal life and productions of Lucille Ball and Desi Arnaz. Some of the things you'll be able to find at the museum include the set that was used for Lucy and Ricky's living room on *I Love Lucy* (which you can see in color for the first time), a set from the *I Love Lucy* Vitameatavegamin episode and a number of other exhibits and artifacts from the late comedian's life and career.

Woodstock Was Held at a Dairy Farm in New York, and You Can Visit the Site Today!

By now, you probably know that Woodstock took place in New York. But did you know that it did *not* take place in the town of Woodstock?

Although the festival planners originally wanted to hold the event in Woodstock, they couldn't find a venue. The festival was later set to take place at an industrial site near Middletown, New York, but that fell through when their permits were revoked.

The festival was saved by a dairy farmer named Max Yasgur, who owned a 600-acre farm in Bethel, New York. Yasgur agreed to allow the festival to be held on his property. The festival didn't take place on his dairy farm, however. It took place on one of his hay fields.

Woodstock is considered the most significant music event of all time. *Rolling Stones* named it as one of the

"50 Moments That Changed the History of Rock and Roll." Some of the musicians and bands who performed include: Janis Joplin, Jimi Hendrix, The Who, Creedence Clearwater Revival, Johnny Winter, Santana, and Joe Cocker.

The festival took place over the course of three days, beginning on August 15th and ending on August 18th, 1969. Though only 200,000 people were expected to attend the festival, there were nearly half a million attendees.

In 2006, the Bethel Woods Center for the Arts opened on the site where Woodstock was held. The Bethel Woods Pavilion hosts outdoor concerts during the months of summer. There's also a museum with exhibits that honor Woodstock, rock and roll, peace and love, and so much more! The Museum at Bethel Woods is open from April to December.

Hip Hop Originated from the Big Apple

Hip hop music is frequently played on the radio today, but have you ever given any thought as to where it all got started?

Hip hop, both as a music genre and a culture, originated from New York City. It all began in the 1970s when young people in the Bronx threw house and block parties in predominantly African-American ghetto neighborhoods. At these parties, DJs would play percussive breaks of songs using a DJ mixer and two turntables. They used techniques such as scratching, beatmatching, and Jamaican toasting, in which they would chant over the beats. It was during this time that rapping was also born.

Early on, the only recorded hip hop was of live shows and mixtapes recorded by DJs. In 1977, DJ Disco Wiz is said to have recorded the first mixed dub recording.

It wasn't until 1979, however, that hip hop was recorded for radio. This was mostly due to lack of acceptance of hip hop out of ghetto neighborhoods. It was also due to a lack of financial resources.

"Rapper's Delight" by the Sugarhill Gang is widely recognized as the first hip hop record, though some consider "King Tim III (Personality Jockey)" by the Fatback Band to be the first. That being said, "Rapper's Delight" was the first to gain mainstream attention and experience commercial success.

Wizard of OZ is Honored in a Town in Upstate New York

Are you a fan of *The Wizard of Oz*? If so, you might want to take a trip to Chittenango in upstate New York. The town is the birthplace of Lyman Frank Baum "L. Frank Baum", author of the book series *The Wonderful Wizard of Oz*.

To honor Baum and his works, the sidewalks are painted like the yellow brick road. Throughout the town, you'll also spot signs of the characters from *Wizard of Oz*.

A number of businesses in the town of Chittenango are *Wizard of Oz* themed. Some of these include Emerald City Lanes Bowling, Tinman Hardware Store, End of the Rainbow Gift Shop, and Auntie Em's Pantry, which is best known for its Oz Cream Cones. There's also an *Oz*-themed casino called the Yellow Brick Road Casino, which is operated by the Oneida Indian tribe.

In downtown Chittenango, you'll also find the All Things Oz Museum. The museum is home to many *Wizard of Oz* themed collectibles, Judy Garland's autograph, props and costumes from the movie, and so much more!

Every year, the town also holds an annual *Wizard of Oz* themed festival called Oz-Stravaganza. The festival generally takes place the first week of June. It features a parade, live shows, and community groups. Special guests often attend the festival. In 2017, one of the special guests was Jane Lahr, daughter of Bert Lahr, the actor who played the "Cowardly Lion". You can even buy one of the bricks from the town's "yellow brick road" to help Chittenango raise money.

Lots of Celebrities Own Restaurants in New York City

Do you want to eat at a restaurant that's owned by one of your favorite celebs? If so, then you've come to the right place. A number of celebrities own restaurants in the Big Apple. Here are some of the most well-known celeb-owned restaurants in NYC:

- Southern Hospitality BBQ: Justin Timberlake pays homage to his Memphis roots at his restaurant in Midtown Manhattan. The casual restaurant has been known to serve up some awesome traditional Southern BBQ. Some celebrities who have appeared at the restaurant include: Channing Tatum and wife Jenna Dewan-Tatum (who re-enacted the iconic dance scene from *Dirty Dancing* at the restaurant), as well as former couple Minka Kelly and Derek Jeter.

- Joanne Trattoria: Lady Gaga and her parents co-own this traditional Italian restaurant in the Upper West Side. The restaurant is named after Lady Gaga's aunt Joanne, who died at seventeen years old from lupus complications.

- The Spotted Pig: Co-owned by Jay-Z, this restaurant serves both British and Italian cuisine. The West Village restaurant is best known for its burgers and sheep's milk ricotta gnudi. Celebrities who frequent the restaurant include: Luke Wilson, David Schwimmer, Jade Law, and Mario Batali.

- Tribeca Grill: This restaurant, which is owned by Robert De Niro, serves up American cuisine and steakhouse food. Other restaurants De Niro co-owns include Nobu and Locanda Verde (where you might spot Mary-Kate Olsen, Gwyneth Paltrow or Bradley Cooper!)

- Mermaid Oyster Bar: Co-owned by *Scrubs* actor Zach Braff, this upscale restaurant in Greenwich Village is known for its East coast oysters and lobster roll.

- Laughing Man Coffee and Tea: Hugh Jackman owns this café, which is all based on the concept of self-sustainability. Its coffee beans are self-sustainability grown in countries such as Peru, Guatemala, Ethiopia, and Papua New Guinea. Located in Tribeca, all profits go to charity.

- Jack's Wife Freda: Co-owned by Piper Perabo of *Coyote Ugly* fame, Jack's Wife Freda is a popular brunch spot. In fact, it's been said to be one of the most common brunch spots people post about on Instagram. With locations in both Soho and the West Village, the bistro is also known for its Israeli-inspired foods.

- SPiN New York: Actress Susan Sarandon co-owns this establishment in Midtown Manhattan.

There are 17 ping-pong tables, a bar, and a restaurant, which is known for its sliders and shared plates. Not only has Kim Kardashian been spotted at SPiN, but Jake Gyllenhaal, David Schwimmer, and other celebs have competed in ping-pong charity events.

The Most Popular Radio Talk Show in the Country Airs From New York City

Did you know the most popular radio talk show in the country airs from New York City?

Elvis Duran and the Morning Show airs live in New York City on the Z100 radio station. The show is now aired on more than 80 other stations, reaching listeners in Philadelphia, Miami, Cleveland, Atlantic City, Fort Myers, New Haven, Richmond, Syracuse, and more.

The radio show, which is hosted by Elvis Duran and his colleagues, reaches 10 million listeners. As of 2018, it is the most-listened-to Top 40 morning program in the entire country.

The show's format has been so successful that other stations have used it as a model. *Elvis Duran and the Morning Show* consists of a celebrity gossip "Entertainment Report", a prank phone call segment called "Phone Taps", song parodies, contests, the occasional celebrity interview, and more.

Friends Fans Can Visit Some of the Show's Landmarks in NYC

If you're a fan of the show *Friends*, then you know landmarks throughout New York City regularly appeared in the show. There are a number of places you can go throughout the city to pay homage to the show, which first aired in 1994.

For starters, you might choose to visit the Pulitzer Fountain, which is featured in the opening credits of *Friends*. The fountain can be found in the Grand Army Plaza. Something you might not know is that the actual fountain was *not* used in the opening credits. What you really see is an exact replica of the fountain.

Although the interior of the characters' apartment building was filmed on-set in Los Angeles, the exterior of the apartment building was shot on the corner of Bedford and Grove in Greenwich Village. Fun fact: it has been estimated that an apartment in the building would cost someone $3.5 million.

Many *Friends* fans want to visit Central Perk, the iconic coffee shop from the show. Unfortunately, the only way to visit a pop-up version of Central Perk (and see that classic orange couch from the show) is to take the Warner Bros. Studio Tour.

NYC Was Once the East Coast's Hollywood

Before the film industry emerged in Hollywood in the early 1930s, New York City was considered to be American film industry central. Many of the major film studios were based in NYC. Paramount Pictures, which is the 2nd oldest film studio in the country and the 5th oldest in the world, was headquartered in the city.

The Return of Sherlock Holmes, *Goodfellas*, and *Carlito's Way* were a few of the many movies that were filmed at Paramount's Kaufman Astoria Studios in Queens. Later on, TV shows like *The Cosby Show*, were shot at the film studio.

Kaufman Astoria Studios is located near the Museum of the Moving Image, the only museum that honors the moving image. It has a collection of over 130,000 artifacts from the TV and film industry. The museum is home to the Jim Henson Exhibit, which is dedicated to the director known for *The Muppet Show*, *Fraggle Rock*, *Sesame Street*, and other classics. The exhibit also contains some of his puppets. If you've ever wanted to see the original puppets used for Kermit the Frog, Miss Piggy, Elmo or Big Bird, then this exhibit is for you.

Kaufman Astoria Studios isn't the only place where filming has taken place in New York City. In fact, Central Park has long been a hotspot for films. It has been featured in more movies than any other location in the entire world!

Romeo and Juliet was the first movie to be filmed in Central Park in 1908. Since then, more than 300 movies had been filmed in the park. Some of the most popular movies to be filmed there include: *When Harry Met Sally, Breakfast at Tiffany's, Home Alone 2: Lost in New York, Ghostbusters, The Avengers, Elf, Maid in Manhattan, Serendipity, Enchanted, 13 Going on 30, Big Daddy, Night at the Museum,* and *Friends with Benefits.*

Gangs of New York is Loosely Based on a True Story

You've probably heard of the movie *Gangs of New York*, but did you know that it's based on a true story?

The movie, starring Leonardo DiCaprio and Daniel Day-Lewis, takes place in the Five Points district of Lower Manhattan in 1863.

It's based on a 1928 nonfiction book called *The Gangs of New York: An Informal History of the Underworld* by Herbert Asbury. The book focuses on several gangs that were prominent in New York City during the 1800s. These included: the Bowery Boys, Plug Uglies, Dead Rabbits, Shirt Tails, and True Blue Americans.

Director Martin Scorsese read the book in 1970 and

believed it would make a good movie. He spent more than twenty years trying to make it happen.

While the book the movie is based on is nonfiction, there has been a lot of controversy over its accuracy. According to a modern historian named Tyler Anbinder, elements of the book were exaggerated. For example, Asbury claimed there was a murder every day in the neighborhood, while Anbinder claims that there was only a murder a month in all of New York City at that time.

A gang fight in the movie that's portrayed as taking place in 1846 is fictional. Meanwhile, the movie leaves out a major fight between the gangs that took place in Five Points in 1857.

The movie depicts Chinese-Americans as a large enough population to have their own community within the neighborhood. While there were Chinese-Americans residing in New York City at the time, it wasn't until 1869 that Chinese immigration to America really increased. The Chinese Theater shown in the movie wasn't built at the time, while the Old Brewery portrayed in the movie had already been demolished during some of the years it had been shown.

While *Gangs of New York* is inspired by actual events, it's important to remember that it's categorized as historical fiction and not 100% accurate.

Many Famous Authors Got Their Start in New York City

Over the years, many authors have moved to New York. Some of them moved in hopes of making connections to get their works published, while others just happened to have success while working other jobs.

Here are some of the most famous American authors of all-time whose careers got started after they moved to the Big Apple:

- Walt Whitman: Known for his collection of poems, Whitman worked in the newspaper industry. He worked as a devil's printer, a typesetter, and even created *The Long Islander* newspaper.

- Harper Lee: The author of *To Kill a Mockingbird* dropped out of college and moved to New York City, where she worked as an airline ticket agent and wrote in her free time. *To Kill a Mockingbird* was written after one of Lee's Broadway composer friends gave her enough money to quit her job and work on a novel for a year.

- Herman Melville: *Moby Dick* author Melville moved to Manhattan for work. Melville worked as a cabin boy on the St. Lawrence merchant ship. The time he spent there inspired his first work, *Redburn: His First Voyage*, along with his other nautical-themed works, including *Moby Dick*.

- Scott Fitzgerald: Best known for *The Great Gatsby* and "The Curious Case of Benjamin Button," Fitzgerald moved to New York City in pursuit of work. He began his career as a journalist before being told to give it up and later became a typist instead.

These are just a few of many authors who got their start in New York City!

The Legend of "Rip Van Winkle" Took Place in the Catskill Mountains of New York

Have you ever heard of the story of "Rip Van Winkle"? In the story, Rip Van Winkle is a Dutch villager who lives in a village at the foothill of the Catskill Mountains. The story begins before the American Revolution takes place.

Rip Van Winkle enjoys the great outdoors, spending time with his friends, and telling stories and repairing toys for the children in town. He doesn't like working, however, which causes his wife to nag him.

To get away from his wife, Rip Van Winkle heads into the woods with his dog one day. He comes across some men who he's never met before and drinks their Dutch gin. Shortly after, he falls asleep.

When Rip Van Winkle wakes up, his dog is gone and he has a foot-long beard. He goes to the local village where people ask him who he voted for. Not knowing the Revolutionary War took place, Rip says he's a supporter of King George III. He almost gets in trouble until an old woman in the town recognizes him as the "long lost" Rip Van Winkle. Rip learns that most of his friends died in the war and also comes across another man named Rip Van Winkle—his son, who is now grown up.

Rip Van Winkle learns that the strange men who he came across in the woods were actually the ghosts of Henry Hudson and his crew. Rip Van Winkle also learns that he was sleeping for at least 20 years.

Although some people believe that the legend of Rip Van Winkle is true, it's not. Author Washington Irving admitted that he had never been to the Catskill Mountains before writing the story.

That being said, an author named Joe Gioia said the story of Rip Van Winkle closely resembles a legend from Seneca Falls, New York. The legend says a squirrel hunter met the elusive "Little People," who he spent one night with. When he returned to his village, he found that all of the people were gone and the village was overgrown by forest. The night he'd spent with the "Little People" had turned into a year.

Sex and the City is Based on a New York City Newspaper Column

Sex and the City is one of the most well-known TV shows set in New York City. The series has even been credited for jumpstarting HBO. Did you know the show is actually based on a newspaper column?

In 1994, Candace Bushnell began writing a column called "Sex and the City" for the *New York Observer*. The humorous column, which ran for two years, was based on both her and her friends' dating experiences.

The first article Candace Bushnell wrote for the column was called "Swingin' Sex? I Don't Think So…." It was about a "couples-only sex club," which Bushnell and her male partner attended and were severely let down. The column featured several lines that went on to be famous quotes from the show.

In 1997, Bushnell's entire column was published in an anthology, which was also called *Sex and the City*. The show would later go on to be based on the book.

Though she initially used her own name, Candace Bushnell later used the name 'Carrie Bradshaw' in her columns for privacy reasons. Bushnell's alter-ego shares her own initials. In the show, Carrie Bradshaw, played by Sarah Jessica Parker, is a writer, too!

A Number of Reality Shows Have Been Filmed in New York

There's no doubt that Americans love their reality TV shows. Did you know that many of your favorite reality shows have been filmed in New York?

Some of the many reality shows that have been filmed in the Empire State include:

- *Judge Judy*
- *America's Next Top Model*
- *Basketball Wives*
- *Project Runway*
- *Newlyweds: The First Year*
- *Mob Wives*
- *The Real Housewives of New York City*
- *Love & Hip Hop*
- *Long Island Medium*
- *Growing Up Gotti*
- *Kourtney & Khloe Take the Hamptons and Kourtney & Kim Take New York*
- *The Apprentice and All-Star Celebrity Apprentice*
- *What Not to Wear*
- *The Real World: New York*
- *The Millionaire Matchmaker*
- *Queer Eye for the Straight Guy*

New York City is Talk Show Central!

If you've always wanted to see a talk show as it's being recorded, then you might want to visit the Big Apple! There are a number of talk shows that are recorded in New York City.

As of 2018, you can be an audience member at one of the following talk shows:

- *The View*
- *The Rachael Ray Show*
- *Dr. Oz*
- *Good Morning America*
- *The Chew*
- *The Daily Show with Trevor Noah*
- *The Tonight Show with Jimmy Fallon*
- *The Late Night Show with Steven Colbert*

The Big Apple is Known as the "Jazz Capital of the World"

If you love jazz music, then you partially have New York City to thank! The Big Apple has long been known as the "jazz capital of the world." A number of jazz music milestones have occurred in NYC.

One of the first successful jazz bands got their start in New York City. That band was the Original Dixieland Jazz Band, and they played in the Big Apple back in

1917.

Cabaret also originated in New York City. It got its start in the 1920s during the prohibition era. It was during this time that bars and nightclubs began to allow musicians to perform. The Cotton Club in Harlem was one of the most famous venues for jazz musicians during that time.

Duke Ellington was a famous bandleader of a jazz orchestra. His orchestra gained national attention after playing at the Cotton Club in Harlem in the mid-1920s.

In 1939, Billie Holiday played her song "Strange Fruit" at Café Society in Greenwich Village. It was the first integrated nightclub at the time.

Stride, which was the first piano style to ever be incorporated into jazz music, originated in NYC.

Jazz music is celebrated every year in New York City at the Winter Jazzfest. Voted as the "#1 Jazz Festival in North America," the festival pays homage to jazz music icons of the past and celebrates the jazz music being made today.

RANDOM FACTS

1. Fran Drescher grew up in Flushing, Queens. The actress went on to star in the hit '90s show *The Nanny* where she played Fran Fine, a nanny from Flushing, Queens who moves to New York's upper East side and falls in love with her wealthy boss.

2. Actress Michelle Trachtenberg was born and raised in Sheepshead Bay in Brooklyn. She later went on to play Georgina in the CW show *Gossip Girl*, which focuses on elite teens who live in the Upper East Side and teens from Brooklyn who struggle to fit in.

3. After dropping out of college, Madonna moved to NYC in 1978 in order to pursue a career in modern dance. When she moved to the city, she worked at Dunkin' Donuts. She was fired after she squirted jelly on a customer.

4. Actress Julia Stiles is a Manhattan native. At eleven years old, she started her acting career with New York's La MaMa Theater Company. Her son, Strummer, was born in 2017 at Mount Sinai hospital in NYC!

5. Lady Gaga, who was born and raised in

Manhattan, honored her home state by doing a remake of Frank Sinatra's song "New York, New York."

6. Lenny Kravitz was born in Manhattan and raised in both Manhattan and Brooklyn. The musician recorded a song about his hometown called "New York City."

7. Barbara Streisand was born and raised in Brooklyn. She went to Erasmus High with fellow musician Neil Diamond! They were in the school choir together and hung out and smoked cigarettes in front of the school.

8. Actor Heath Ledger, who is best-known for his role in his final film *The Dark Knight*, was found dead in an apartment in Manhattan in 2008.

9. Vanessa Williams, who was born and raised in the Bronx, won Miss New York in 1983. She was recognized as the first African-American woman to ever win Miss America, but she was later pressured to give up the title after *Penthouse* published unauthorized nude photos of her. Williams has since gone on to have success in singing and acting.

10. *Sesame Street*, which is the longest-running television series for kids, is filmed in Astoria, Queens. The set is designed to capture the feel of different neighborhoods throughout NYC.

11. Mariah Carey was born in Huntington, New York. She is currently a resident of New York City. Her grandfather immigrated from New York to Venezuela and adopted the last name, Carey.

12. The show *Will & Grace* featured several famous buildings throughout New York City. The roommates lived at 155 Riverside Drive, while the location of Grace's design studio was in the Puck Building.

13. Taylor Swift paid $18 million for a townhouse located in the Tribeca neighborhood of Lower Manhattan. It's located next to her penthouse.

14. Christina Aguilera was born in Staten Island. Though her family was forced to move to New Jersey, Texas, Japan, and other locations because her father was in the military, the musician can always be found in NYC at Madame Tussauds wax museum.

15. Musicians Alicia Keys and Jay-Z, who are both NYC natives, paid homage to their home state in their song "Empire State of Mind."

16. Sean Combs, who has been known as Puff Daddy, P. Diddy, and many other nicknames, was born in Harlem. He was raised in Mount Vernon, NY. Combs began his career as an intern at Uptown Records in New York. Combs later

went on to become a talent director at the record company. During that time, he played a role in developing Jodeci and Mary J. Blige.

17. A number of songs have been written about New York City. Some of these include: "Living for the City" by Stevie Wonder, "No Sleep Till Brooklyn" by the Beastie Boys, "Guaranteed Raw" by the Notorious B.I.G., "Visions of Johanna" by Bob Dylan, "Black Jesus + Amen Fashion" by Lady Gaga, "Spanish Harlem" by Ben E. King, "I Am... I Said" by Neil Diamond, "Mona Lisas and Mad Hatters" by Elton John, and "14th Street" by Rufus Wainwright.

18. Actress/musician Jennifer Lopez was born and raised in the Bronx. She announced this to the world in her song "Jenny from the Block." Lopez has said that growing up in the Bronx has influenced everything about her.

19. Cyndi Lauper was born and raised in Queens, New York. In the early '70s, the musician performed with a number of cover bands. One of the bands she was in, Flyer, was popular throughout the New York metro area.

20. All four members of the Beatles have performed at Madison Square Gardens, but the band never performed there together. In 1974, John Lennon gave his second to last performance at MSG.

Test Yourself – Questions and Answers

1. Which hit '90s TV show was *not* set in New York?

   a. Friends
   b. The Nanny
   c. Boy Meets World

2. Which genre of music got its start in New York City?

   a. Hip hop
   b. Country
   c. Blues

3. Which city in New York celebrates Lucille Ball's life every year?

   a. Huntington
   b. Jamestown
   c. Manhattan

4. Who is the DJ behind the New York-based radio talk show that's one of the most popular in the country?

   a. Ryan Seacrest
   b. Mark Larson
   c. Elvis Duran

5. Which female musician is *not* from New York?

   a. Alicia Keys
   b. Mariah Carey
   c. Beyoncé

Answers

1. c.

2. a.

3. b.

4. c.

5. c.

CHAPTER THREE

FACTS ABOUT NEW YORK CITY'S ATTRACTIONS

Whether you're thinking about visiting New York City or you already have, you may have never considered the history of some of its most popular tourist attractions. For example, do you know which architect designed the Statue of Liberty? Do you know who started the annual New Year's Eve bash in Times Square? Did you know there's a place in the city where couples can feel "sparks fly" when they kiss?

The Statue of Liberty Has a Full Name

Even though most of us only know her as the Statue of Liberty, the statue actually has a full name! It's "Liberty Enlightening the World."

How did the statue get its name? It came from the statue's torch, which is a symbol of enlightenment. According to the National Park Service, the torch "lights the way to freedom showing us the path to liberty."

Unfortunately, the statue's torch isn't the same torch it was originally built with. The original torch was damaged in the Black Tom explosion on July 30th, 1916. The explosion, which was a German act of sabotage to destroy American-made ammunition that was going to be supplied to the USA's allies during World War I, left the Statue of Liberty with $100,000 worth of damage. Due to structural damages caused by the explosion, the torch hasn't been open to the public ever since.

In 1986, a newly constructed replacement torch was added to the statue. Its flame, which is made of copper, is covered in 24k gold. During the daytime, the gold reflects the sun's rays. At nighttime, the torch glows due to its lights.

The original torch can be found in the lobby of the Statue of Liberty.

Central Park is Designed to Represent the State of New York

With 42 million visitors a year, Central Park is one of the most bustling places in all of New York City. The park, which was the first public park to ever be landscaped in America, spans across 843 acres of land and 3.5 square miles. Whether you've been to

Central Park or not, here's a fact that you probably don't know about it: the park was designed to resemble New York state.

The park, which was designed by Frank Olmstead, is meant to be a mini-scale representation of New York. The south side of Central Park was designed to give off a more elite, less woodsy feel. This area of the park is meant to represent New York City.

As you enter the northern part of the park, you'll notice more hills and woods. This rustic area also contains more benches and gazebos. This area of the park is supposed to remind you of the Catskills and the Adirondack Mountains.

Broadway's Longest-Running Show Isn't Its Highest Earning

Whether you've always dreamt of going to a Broadway show or if you already frequent them, you may be wondering which show has been around the longest and which has earned the most money. You might be surprised to learn that they are *not* one in the same!

The longest-running Broadway show is *The Phantom of the Opera*. The show first made its Broadway premiere back in 1988. Since then, it has run more than 11,000 times. The show is still running today. *Chicago* is the second-longest running Broadway show. Since it opened in 1996, *Chicago* has run more than 7,000 times and continues to run to date. Neither of these shows has been the highest-earning Broadway show, however.

The highest-earning Broadway show is *Lion King*, which has grossed a whopping $1.09 billion. *The Phantom of the Opera* is the second highest earner, hitting $850 million. The third highest earner is *Wicked*, with earnings of $477 million.

The Empire State Building May be More Romantic Than You Thought

The Empire State Building was built at a time when builders were in a race to build the world's highest skyscraper. Unveiled in 1931, the Empire State Building was the world's tallest landscaper. It maintained that title until 1970 when the first World Trade Center tower was built.

Since the Empire State Building was built, more than 30 people have committed suicide by jumping from the building.

When it comes to romance, the Empire State Building might not be the first place that comes to mind. However, it might be one of the most romantic spots in the city. In fact, couples see "sparks fly" here— *literally*.

Some couples have noticed sparks fly—and the

feeling of being jolted—when they kiss at the top of the Empire State Building. This is due to static electricity at the top of the building.

You can even get married at the Empire State Building. If you want to have your wedding here, you'll have to do it on Valentine's Day, though, as this is the only day of the year when weddings are allowed on the building. Weddings are held in the form of a contest, however. In 2017, 13 lucky couples were chosen to hold their weddings or vow renewal on the 86th Floor Observatory.

There's also an Empire State Building Wedding Club for people who have their wedding at the Empire State Building. This grants them free entry into the observatory on Valentine's Day every year.

The Rockefeller Center Christmas Tree Topper is Massive!

Sure, you know the Rockefeller Center Christmas Tree is huge. But have you ever given any thought to how big the tree topper is?

The Swarovski star that tops the tree is a whopping 550 pounds. It's 9.5 feet in diameter and is made up of 25,000 crystals. There are also 1,024 programmable channels to ensure that the star keeps twinkling.

You might be wondering how that 550-pound star stays on top of the tree. The tree weighs enough to support the weight of the topper.

To put things into perspective, the 2017 Rockefeller Center Christmas Tree was 75 feet tall and weighed 24,000 pounds. This wasn't even the largest Christmas Tree that's been displayed at Rockefeller Center. In 1999, the tree, which came from a farm in Killingworth, Connecticut, stood 100 feet tall (though that tree only weighed 14,000 pounds).

So, how much is the Rockefeller Center Christmas Tree topper worth? Although the Swarovski star's value has been kept a secret, it's estimated to be worth more than $1.5 million.

One World Trade Center is 1,776 Feet Tall for a Reason

One World Trade Center is the rebuilt World Trade Center. It was named after the North Tower, one of the two towers on the World Trade Center that were destroyed during the terrorist attacks on September 11th, 2001.

Here's something you might not know about One World Trade Center. The reason it was built to stand 1,776 feet tall is an intentional reference to the year the Declaration of Independence was signed. The United States has been known to hide references to the Declaration of Independence in other places, such as the dollar bill.

With its height, One World Trade Center is often considered to be the tallest building in the United States, but some beg to differ. The Willis Tower in Chicago, which stands 1,451 feet high, still holds the national record as the world's tallest building. How can this be? Well, a spire was added to One World Trade Center to ensure it hit 1,776 feet tall. Without the spire, One World Trade Center stands at only 1,368 feet tall—making it technically shorter than the Willis Tower.

Regardless of whether or not it's the tallest building in America, One World Trade Center was built with careful planning to memorialize the lives lost in 9/11. The building is also located just north of the National September 11 Memorial & Museum, which was built where the original World Trade Center once stood.

The First New Year's Eve Bash in Times Square Was Thrown by a New York City Newspaper Company

Today, nearly a million people ring in the New Year in Times Square. Even when not in attendance, many people throughout the country watch the ball drop live from Times Square on *Dick Clark's New Year's Rockin' Eve* with Ryan Seacrest. In 2018, the TV program drew 15.7 million viewers. Have you ever given any thought to how the tradition of celebrating New Year's in Times Square got started?

The first New Year's Eve celebration in Times Square was held by the *New York Times*. The newspaper company hosted the event to celebrate its opening in 1903. Fireworks were shot off to ring in the New Year. About 200,000 people were in attendance the first year. By 1904, the popularity of the event grew.

The ball was introduced in 1907. Replacing the fireworks show that had been held in previous years, the electrically-lit ball was lowered on a flagpole when the clock struck midnight to ring in the year of 1908.

The Times Square Ball has dropped every year since 1908, with the exception of 1942 and 1943. The celebration was not held during those years due to wartime blackouts.

Since the introduction of the Times Squares Ball, it's come a long way! Back in 1907, the ball contained 100 light bulbs and was lowered on a 141-foot pole. The ball that's dropped down a 475-foot pole today in Times Square has a computerized LED multi-colored lighting system and reflective crystal panels.

Dick Clark began to host *Dick Clark's New Year's Rockin' Eve* in 1972. He created the program with a younger audience in mind. At the time, there was another program run by Guy Lombardo. Clark was well-known as the host of *American Bandstand*. *Dick Clark's New Year's Rockin' Eve* grew in popularity, especially once Guy Lombardo died.

Dick Clark's New Year's Rockin' Eve is under contract to air on ABC until at least 2024.

Coney Island Was Probably Named After Rabbits

Have you ever wondered where Coney Island got its name? No one knows for sure, but there are a few theories.

The Lenape tribes are said to have called the island "the island without shadows." When the Dutch settled on the island, they renamed it *"Konijnen Eiland,"* the Dutch term for "Rabbit Island," due to the large population of rabbits on the sandy island.

Some theorists believe the island may be named after "Conyn," which may have been one of the surnames among early Dutch settlers. Others believe it may be named after John Coleman, one of Henry Hudson's crew members who was killed by Native Americans. Overall, however, the rabbit island theory is the most widely believed.

Madison Square Garden Has Hosted Some of the Biggest Benefit Concerts of All-Time

Benefit concerts have become a popular way to raise money for tragedies and natural disasters. Did you know that Madison Square Garden has hosted some of the highest-earning benefit concerts of all-time?

In fact, the MSG arena was the first to host a benefit concert when it held "The Concert for Bangladesh." The event took place in 1971 and raised money for Bangladeshi refugees after the Bangladesh Liberation War-related genocide. Forty thousand people came out to see former Beatle member Ringo Starr, Eric Clapton, Bob Dylan, Leon Russell, Billy Preston, and Badfinger perform, raising nearly $250,000 for Bangladesh relief. Albums from the event were also sold, which raised an additional $12 million.

"The Concert for New York City" also took place at Madison Square Garden. In addition to raising money, the concert was also used as a way to honor the first responders and lives lost in the terror attacks. The concert, which was aired live on VH1, raised over $35 million. More than 60 performers participated in the event, including: Bon Jovi, Elton John, Jay-Z, Destiny's Child, the Backstreet Boys, and Adam Sandler. Performers also autographed memorabilia, which earned an extra $275,000.

"From the Big Apple to the Big Easy" was a benefit concert that was held at Madison Square Garden, in collaboration with nearby Radio City Music Hall. The benefit was held for Hurricane Katrina relief efforts. The concerts from: Elton John, Bette Midler, Jimmy Buffett, Elvis Costello, and other performers helped raise approximately $9 million for the cause.

The largest benefit concert to ever be held (both at MSG and of all-time) was "12-12-12: The Concert for Sandy Relief." The event raised $60 million for the victims of the hurricane, with $30 million of that being raised from ticket sales alone. The concert was aired live on 39 TV stations, streamed on more than 25 websites, and broadcasted on more than 50 radio stations. Performances were given by: Paul McCartney, Kanye West, Alicia Keys, Bon Jovi, The Who, Bruce Springsteen, Billy Joel, Eric Clapton, and the Rolling Stones.

Central Park Zoo Animals Were Featured in the First Ever Macy's Day Parade

Watching the Macy's Thanksgiving Day Parade has become a pastime for many Americans. You might be surprised to learn the very first Macy's parade was much different from the one that takes place in the streets of Manhattan today.

The parade was originally called the "Macy's Christmas Parade" when it first made its debut on Thanksgiving Day in 1924. The parade was held to celebrate the expansion of the Macy's store in Manhattan. As you can probably guess, the parade was Christmas-themed. What you might not guess is that there were no balloons in the first Macy's Day Parade. Live animals were used instead!

The animals included goats, camels, donkeys, and

elephants. These animals came from the Central Park Zoo. Horses were also used to pull the floats.

Live animals were used in 1925 and 1926, as well. Lions, tigers, and bears were included in the parade those years. However, the animals scared the children who were watching the parade. As a result, the parade stopped using animals.

In 1927, Macy's introduced its giant helium balloons in place of animals. The very first balloons that year included Felix the Cat, Toy Soldier, The Dragon, and The Elephant. It was also renamed "Macy's Thanksgiving Day Parade" the same year.

Grand Central Terminal Was Saved by a Former First Lady

Grand Central Terminal is one of New York City's most famous landmarks. It's been featured in everything from the movie *Avengers* to the first episode of the show *Gossip Girl*. But did you know the terminal would have been destroyed if it weren't for a former First Lady?

In 1975, there were plans to destroy Grand Central Terminal to make room for the railroad. When Jackie Kennedy Onassis read about these plans in the *New York Times*, she was outraged. The terminal meant a lot to the former First Lady. She saw it as symbolic of Manhattan, a city her grandfather had helped build.

After Onassis read about the city's plans to destroy Grand Central, she fought against it with the Municipal Art Society. The Municipal Art Society was a well-respected group that had previously been involved with the creation of the city's first zoning code, planned the subway lines, and the development of the Landmarks Preservation Law in 1965.

Jackie Kennedy Onassis played a key role in saving Grand Central. She was the highlight speaker at a press conference about the plans. Onassis also wrote a letter to New York Mayor Abraham Beame asking him to preserve the city's beauty and history by stopping the plans from going through. Mayor Beame announced that he would appeal the plans a week after receiving her letter.

Staten Island Ferries Were Once Used for More Than Transporting People

Between 2014 and 2015, 22 million people rode on the Staten Island Ferry! But did you know that Staten Island's ferries weren't always used just for transportation?

During the Civil War, the Union army used ferry boats from all over the country. The ferries they purchased from Staten Island—the Clifton and Westfield—were used as gunships, fully equipped with cannons. They were considered to be some of the best used in the war. While they were not used on a long-term basis, they were very useful.

In 1863, the Westfield was destroyed in a surprise attack from the Confederates. The ship was blown in half and the crew was killed. Remains of the ship could be seen off the coast of Galveston for years, serving as a reminder of the Confederate defeat.

In 1987, ferries from Staten Island served another purpose. Due to prison overcrowding on Rikers Island, Mayor Ed Koch came up with a plan to turn two former ferries into prison barges. The ferries held more than 300 prisoners off the coast of the Bronx. The ships were used by the Department of Corrections until 1997.

Many Sculptures Can be Found in Central Park

Central Park is home to a number of sculptures. Most of these sculptures were donated to the park by organizations or people. Here's a list of some of the most popular sculptures you'll find there:

- *Alice in Wonderland* is, by far, the most popular statue that can be found in Central Park. The sculpture features: Alice, the White Rabbit, the Mad Hatter, the Cheshire Cat, and the dormouse. Created by Jose de Creeft and added to the park in 1959, the sculpture attracts many children.

- *Ludwig van Beethoven* is a sculpture that was created in honor of the late composer by German-American sculptor Henry Baerer. The statue was added to Central Park in 1884.

- *Hans Christian Anderson* features the famous fairy-tale writer sitting and reading to a duck, in honor of his most famous story "The Ugly Duckling." The sculpture was created by Georg J. Lober in 1956.

- *Still Hunt* is a sculpture that was created by Edward Kemeys. Added to Central Park in 1863, the sculpture features a cougar on a rock ledge about to pounce. The sculpture has scared many joggers.

- *The Angel of the Waters*, otherwise known as the Bethesda Fountain, is located at the center of the lower terrace. Sculpted by Emma Stebbins, the sculpture was unveiled when Central Park was completed in 1873. It's the only sculpture in the park that was commissioned by the city of New York.

- *Group of Bears* is a bronze and granite sculpture of three bears. Created by Paul Howard Manship, the statue was unveiled to the park in 1990.

- *William Shakespeare* is a bronze statue of the late poet on a stone pedestal. Sculpted by John Quincy Adams Ward, the statue was added to the park in 1872.

- *Dancing Goat* and *Honey Bear* are two statues created by Frederick George Richard Roth. Both are fountains in the Central Park Zoo and were installed in 1937.

- *Seventh Regiment Memorial* honors the lives lost from that regiment during the Civil War. The park became home to the statue is 1874.

- *Christopher Columbus* is a replica of a sculpture created by Jeronimo Suñol in Madrid. The replica was added to the park in 1892.

- *Eagles and Prey* is the oldest sculpture of any New York City park. Created by Christophe Fatin in 1853, the statue was added to the park in 1863. The sculpture depicts a goat that's about to be devoured by two eagles.

- *Untermyer Fountain* is a bronze cast of Walter Schott's sculpture, *Three Dancing Maidens*. It was donated to the park by the Untermyer family in 1940.

- *Alexander Hamilton* is a granite sculpture that honors the American founding father. Commissioned by Hamilton's son, the statue was sculpted by Carl Conrads and donated to the park in 1880.

- *Balto* is a statue that honors the sled dog who

led his team through a snowstorm in 1925 to deliver medication that stopped a diphtheria outbreak. Sculpted by Frederick George Richard Roth, the statue was added to the park the same year of the storm.

- The *Burnett Memorial Fountain* was created by Bessie Potter Vonnoh between the years of 1926 and 1936. The sculpture, which was placed in the Conservatory Garden, was designed as a storytelling memorial in memory of author Frances Hodgson Burnett. It's believed the boy and girl in the sculpture are Mary and Dicken, from Burnett's famous book *The Secret Garden*.

- *Indian Hunter* depicts a Native American hunting with a wolf. Sculpted by John Quincy Adams Ward, the sculpture was added to the park in 1866.

- The *107th Infantry Memorial* is a monument that pays homage to the men who served in the infantry regiment of the same name during World War I. It was created by Karl Illava, who served as a sergeant in the Infantry Regiment. The memorial was added to the park in 1927.

- *Simón Bolívar* can be seen riding a horse in a sculpture overlooking Central Park West. The sculpture sits where the Bolivar Hotel once stood.

- The *King Jagiello Monument* depicts the King Wladyslaw II Jagiello of Poland and Grand Duke of Lithuania on a horse. The statue, which sits on a tall pedestal, is considered to be one of the most impressive statues in all of Central Park. It was added to the park in 1945.

A total of 22 statues depicting historical figures can be found throughout the park. All of these statues are of men.

The Bronx Zoo is the Largest Metropolitan Zoo

Did you know the Bronx Zoo is the largest metropolitan zoo in the United States? The zoo is set on 265 acres of land!

When it opened on November 8th, 1899, the zoo was home to 843 animals and exhibits. Today, you can see more than 6,000 animals from more than 600 species.

Since it first opened to the public, the Bronx Zoo has accomplished some of the "firsts" in the zoo world.

In 1901, the Wildlife Conservation's first veterinary department was formed at the Bronx Zoo. In 1916, the zoo also opened the first fully equipped animal hospital.

An exhibit called "Lion Island" was opened in 1940. It was the first exhibit in the country that allowed animals in the African Plains habitat to wander without a cage.

The Bronx Zoo opened the African Plains Exhibit in 1941. It was the first exhibit that allowed visitors to view predator and prey in a naturalistic setting.

The zoo opened the world's first nocturnal animals exhibit. The exhibit, which was called "The World of Darkness," ran until 2009.

The New York Public Library is Home to a Number of Odd Artifacts

The New York Public Library is the second largest library in the United States, second only to the Library of Congress. It's the fourth largest library in the entire world. It's home to a lot of books—53 million, to be exact—but did you know a number of other surprising artifacts can be found at the New York Public Library?

For starters, you can find locks of hair from a number of famous people throughout history. Some of these include: Wild Bill Hickok, Charlotte Bronte, and Walt Whitman. The locks of hair are signed and dated.

Charles Dickens' favorite letter-opener can be found in one of the library collections. The shaft is made of ivory, but the handle is the embalmed paw of Dickens' cat, Bob.

The original stuffed animals the Winnie-the-Pooh stories were written about can also be found at the New York Public Library. Winnie-the-Pooh, Piglet,

Eeyore, Tigger, and Kanga have called the library home since 1987.

These are just a few of the many odd artifacts you'll find at the New York Public Library!

Random Facts

1. The Statue of Liberty used to be dark brown in color, but its copper exterior has since turned green. While this is caused by deterioration, the green coating also protects the statue from seeing any further damage—meaning, the statue's green color is here to stay!

2. Although the Empire State Building falls within the boundaries of Manhattan's zip code, the building has its own zip code! In 1980, it got the zip code of 10118.

3. The Bronx Zoo is the largest metropolitan zoo in the entire United States. It houses more than 4,000 animals and 500 species.

4. Times Square wasn't called that at first. It was named after the *New York Times* when the world-famous newspaper moved there in 1904. Prior to that, Times Square was known as Longacre Square.

5. Despite the fact that the American Museum of Natural History is home to one of the best dinosaur collections in the entire world, most of its fossils remain in storage.

6. The Macy's Thanksgiving Day Parade was put on hiatus during World War II due to a shortage of rubber and helium. It stopped in 1942 and

resumed in 1945. The following year, its route was cut in half.

7. The Statue of Liberty was sculpted by Frédéric Auguste Bartholdi. It has been said that the statue's face was modeled after Bartholdi's mother. Gustave Eiffel, who was the architect behind the Eiffel Tower in Paris, built the Statue of Liberty. The Statue of Liberty gets fewer visitors than the Eiffel Tower does. In 2016, the Statue of Liberty had 4.5 million visitors, while the Eiffel Tower had 7 million.

8. St. Patrick's Cathedral, which is a National Historic Landmark, is the largest Gothic Roman Catholic Cathedral in all of America. The cathedral sees 5 million visitors each year—more than the Statue of Liberty!

9. Radio City Music Hall is connected to Rockefeller Center through a secret underground tunnel. It was previously used by commuters and then as a general admission seating entrance for schools and large groups. Today, it's used by the performers as a private entrance to the music hall. Almost all performers use the tunnel to avoid the Paparazzi.

10. Brooklyn Botanic Garden opened one of the first children's gardening programs in 1914. There are still garden programs offered for kids today!

11. One of the most famous trees in all of New York City can be found in Prospect Park. The elm tree, which has been named Camperdown Elm, was transplanted from Scotland to Prospect Park. The tree has gained so much popularity due to how its branches grow parallel to the ground. While the tree almost died in the 1960s, it was able to be preserved. It can be found today behind the Prospect Park Boathouse.

12. The movie *Night at the Museum* is based on a fictional book that takes place at the American Museum of Natural History. Though the interior scenes in the movie were shot in Vancouver, the exterior scenes were shot at the actual museum. This isn't the only time the American Museum of Natural History has been featured in film, either! Ross Geller in *Friends* worked at the museum at one point during the show. The AMNH also appears in *The Devil Wears Prada* and *K-Pax*.

13. Mickey Mouse didn't debut in the Macy's Thanksgiving Day Parade until 1934! Macy's designers worked personally with Walt Disney to create the balloon, which was held down by 25 people. Surprisingly, Mickey isn't the character who's appeared in the parade most often! That would be Snoopy, who first premiered in the parade in 1968 and has had a total of 39 appearances. However, Snoopy was replaced by

Charlie Brown in 2016.

14. The Brooklyn Bridge is said to be the inspiration for more art than any other manmade structure in America. The bridge has been painted by Georgia O'Keeffe, Andy Warhol, and other famous artists. It's also been the focus of photographers, poets, musicians, filmmakers, and more.

15. Sea-Lion Park, the first enclosed amusement park in the United States, was opened on Coney Island in 1895 by Captain Paul Boyton. Boyton, who was famous for being an aquatic daredevil, did one thing differently when he opened Sea-Lion Park. He enclosed it with a fence. He also charged a single admission fee, which was something that had never been done before. Some of the attractions included a water chute and an aquatics shower. Sea-Lion Park was later replaced by Luna Park in 1903.

16. Times Square has a free visitor center and museum, which is located in the Embassy Theater. The Embassy Theater, which is the world's first newsreel theater, was the only theater in the United States that was once managed and run by women only. At the museum, you'll see some of the costumes used in Broadway productions, learn about the history of Times Square, and write a wish on confetti that will be released when the ball drops on New Year's Eve.

17. If you're not that into art, you won't want to skip out on a visit to the Metropolitan Museum of Art. The oldest surviving piano can be found at the museum—along with approximately 5,000 other instruments that can be found at the MET. The museum also has an Arms and Armor department, where you'll find Henry VIII's armor and other historical battle gear. More than 35,000 historically significant pieces of clothing and accessories can be found at the MET's Costume Institute. You'll also find an Egyptian temple, Chinese Garden Court, a 16th-century Spanish patio, and so much more.

18. Bryant Park sits above some literary masterpieces. In 1989, the New York Public Library built a space beneath the park for additional storage. Currently, 40 miles of bookshelves can be found beneath Bryant Park. It's been estimated that there's enough space underneath the park to store 3.2 million books and 50,000 reels of film.

19. Everyone from the Beatles and Judy Garland to Billie Holiday has performed at Carnegie Hall, but the first composer to ever perform at the music hall was Tchaikovsky. Tchaikovsky performed on April 5th, 1891, which was opening night. Maestro Walter Damrosch knew they needed a big-name performer to make the

music hall succeed. Tchaikovsky traveled to America from Russia and conducted five of his pieces at the hall.

20. There's an area in the city known as "Little Britain." Situated in the West Village, there's a corner that's unofficially known as "Little Britain Boulevard." One of the most popular businesses in Little Britain is Tea & Sympathy, a restaurant serving traditional British tea and cuisine ranging from scones to Shepherd's pie. A Salt & Battery is a popular fish and chips restaurant in the area. A little shop called Carry On sells traditional British loose and bagged tea.

Test Yourself – Questions and Answers

1. What is the Statue of Liberty's full name?

   a. Liberty Enlightening the World
   b. Liberty of the World
   c. Liberty Freedom of the World

2. What is the longest-running Broadway show?

   a. Lion King
   b. Wicked
   c. The Phantom of the Opera

3. Which New York City attraction has the highest number of visitors a year?

   a. St. Patrick's Cathedral
   b. Central Park
   c. The Statue of Liberty

4. Which former First Lady saved Grand Central Terminal from destruction?

   a. Jackie Kennedy Onassis
   b. Michelle Obama
   c. Hillary Clinton

5. The first Times Square New Year's Eve bash was thrown by who?

   a. The New York Observer
   b. The New York Times
   c. The New York Post

Answers

1. a.

2. c.

3. b

4. a.

5. b.

CHAPTER FOUR

NEW YORK INVENTIONS, IDEAS, AND MORE!

Have you ever wondered what inventions have come out of New York? New York has been the origin of a number of foods, products, and other inventions that you use on a day to day basis! Read on to learn more about some of the things that started in New York!

Pizza

It's often said that you haven't tasted pizza until you've tried pizza in New York, and for good reason! Pizza got its start in NYC.

While pizza originated from Italy, Americans can thank New York City for the pizza they eat today. Lombardi's, which is located in the Little Italy section of Manhattan, was the first pizzeria to open in the United States. The pizzeria opened in 1905.

Lombardi's first served pizza that was cooked with wood fires. However, in 1905, the owner of

Lombardi's served the first coal-fired pizza. Although it's illegal to cook a pizza that way, Lombardi's and other pizzerias throughout the city still use coal ovens during their pizza-cooking process.

Since then, pizza has come a long way! Now, pizzerias across the country serve a variety of different types of pizza, ranging from New York-style and deep-dish pizza to stuffed crust pizza and pizza bagels.

So, what exactly sets a New York-style pizza apart from other pizzas? Well, several things. For starters, NY-style pies are wide, hand-tossed, and have thin crust. It's meant to be folded into a V. New York-style pizza is always made from fresh mozzarella, and there's never an overabundance of tomato sauce.

Toilet Paper

Today, many of us take toilet paper for granted. Have you ever wondered who you should thank for its invention?

Joseph Gayetty began selling toilet paper in 1857 in New York City. He marketed it as "medicated paper for the water-closet." At the time, his toilet paper was made of Manilla hemp paper, which contained aloe for lubrication. It was intended to help prevent hemorrhoids. His toilet paper was sold throughout the 1920s.

Despite the fact that Gayetty has been credited with

inventing American toilet paper, the first patent for toilet paper and toilet paper dispensers was issued to Seth Wheeler of Albany, New York.

It took a long time for toilet paper to be perfect. In the 1930s, people were still getting splinters from their toilet paper!

Hot Dogs and Hamburgers

Ever wonder where hot dogs and hamburgers came from? It's what Americans eat to celebrate their independence on the Fourth of July, but where did these foods come from? Both of these all-American foods originated in New York City!

While hot dogs weren't invented in the United States, American hot dogs got their start on Coney Island. This isn't surprising, considering a trip to Coney Island is incomplete without stopping at Nathan's Famous hot dogs. But did you know that Nathan's wasn't the first Coney Island hot dog stand?

A German immigrant named Charles Feltman has been credited with inventing hot dogs on a bun (though his original "hot dogs" were actually pork sausages on a bun). Feltman originally started out his business in 1867 in the form of a push-cart stand. His hot dogs came to be known as Coney Island's red hots and sold for ten cents. Feltman later opened a restaurant, along with an entire empire that took up a street of the seaside town.

In 1916, one of Feltman's former employees changed everything. Nathan Handwerker, a Polish-American, was encouraged by his friends Eddie Cantor and Jimmy Durante to open a competing business. Handwerker saved up $300 and opened his own hot dog stand called Nathan's Famous. He used his wife Ida's hot dog recipe and sold the hot dogs for five cents each. Before long, his hot dogs were the most popular on Coney Island and began to gain popularity through the rest of the United States.

The story of how hamburgers came to be is a little less clear. It has been said that in the 1820s, restaurants throughout New York City began to serve Hamburg-style steak in a bowl with breadcrumbs and onions. The idea was to draw German immigrants, who journeyed to America from Hamburg. Eventually, restaurants began to serve Hamburg-style steak on bread and named it the "hamburger."

The Bloody Mary

Have you ever wondered who invented the Bloody Mary cocktail?

The origin of the Bloody Mary isn't entirely known. Here's what we *do* know: in the United States, the cocktail got its start in New York City. What we don't know for sure is who actually invented the drink.

A bartender named Henry Zbikiewicz at New York's 21 Club claimed that he invented the cocktail in the 1930s.

However, Fernand Petiot claimed that he invented the Bloody Mary in the early 1920s. At the time, he was working at the New York Bar in Paris, France, which was frequented by Ernest Hemingway. The bar, which was later renamed Harry's New York Bar, claimed the drink was created at the spur of the moment. He then said he began to make the drink New York's St. Regis Hotel's King Cole Role. In 1964, he told *The New Yorker* his secret recipe. He also said the hotel was serving 100-150 Blood Mary's every day.

So, who invented the Bloody Mary in the USA? Who knows. All we know is that it did come from New York City.

General Tso's Chicken

It's a popular item on Chinese food menus across the United States, but do you know how General Tso's chicken started out?

Although there are several claims circulating out there involving the creation of General Tso's chicken, Peng's Restaurant on East 44th Street in New York claims that it was the first to serve the menu item.

It all started with a Taiwanese chef named Peng

Chang-Kuei. Peng was forced to flee Taiwan during the Chinese Civil War.

In the 1990s, Peng opened a restaurant in Hunan, a province in China. He included General Tso's as a menu item. However, the local people found the recipe too sweet. Peng later closed the restaurant.

Peng later moved to New York where he opened Peng's in 1973. After he added sugar to his original General Tso's recipe, the menu item became a hit! A 1977 review of Peng's General Tso chicken called it "a stir-fried masterpiece."

It has long been rumored that General Tso's chicken was a favorite of General Tso of the Qing Dynasty. However, there is nothing to prove whether or not that this is actually true.

Air Conditioning

Willis Carrier created the "Apparatus for Treating Air" in 1902. However, his system wasn't created for people! The "Apparatus for Treating Air" was originally designed to prevent the humidity from causing the paper to warp at a printing company in Bushwick, Brooklyn. It was an added bonus that the workers were kept comfortable in the summer heat.

Prior to Carrier's invention, people used to wrap buildings in cloth soaked in melted ice water with a fan that blew hot air. While this cooling method was effective, it wasn't practical as it required more than 250,000 pounds of ice each month.

ATMs

The first money-dispensing device was introduced in New York in 1939 by Luther George Simjian. The contraption was called the Bankograph. Simjian convinced the City Bank of New York—which is today's Citibank—to test his invention for six months.

Surprisingly, the first ATM didn't go over too well. Unlike today's ATMs, the Bankograph didn't dispense cash. It only accepted coins, cash, and checks. Due to lack of customer acceptance, the Bank of New York didn't use the Bankograph past the trial period. The bank claimed the only ones using the device were prostitutes and gamblers.

While Simjian is credited with developing the ATM, the first ATM with cash features would later go on to be developed in the United Kingdom.

Credit Cards

Most of us can't live without credit cards. Wondering who to thank for those late fees or all that credit card debt? You can blame it all on John Biggins, a banker and credit promoter at the Flatbush National Bank in Brooklyn.

In 1946, Biggins created the "Charg-It" program, which allowed local retailers to offer credit to bank customers. The bank would pay the retailers and then collect the debt owed from the cardholders. The program, which was the first of its kind, would later be accepted throughout the country.

Potato Chips

Have you ever given any thought to who invented potato chips? The inventor of one of America's favorite junk foods goes to George Crum, the head chef at a restaurant in Saratoga Springs, New York called Moon's Lake House.

Potato chips were born in 1853 when one of the people dining at the restaurant was unsatisfied with how thick Crum's french fries were. The customer also claimed the fries were too moist and didn't have enough salt.

In an attempt at insulting the customer, Crum sliced up some really thin potatoes, fried them to a crisp, and drenched them in salt. The customer ended up loving the invention, leading to "Saratoga Chips."

George Crum later went on to meet Herman Lay—the same Herman Lay who would go on to become co-founder of the Frito-Lay company. The rest is history!

Christmas

Did you know that Christmas the way it's celebrated in the United States today came from New York? Obviously, Christmas itself didn't originate from New York. However, the idea of a commercialized Christmas involving giving gifts did.

A little-known fact is that Christmas was once banned in the United States by the Puritans in 1659. People were actually forced to (gasp) work during the Christmas holiday. People who were caught celebrating or feasting were even fined five shillings.

In the early 1800s, early settlers of New York City (which at the time was New Amsterdam) decided to bring back the Dutch tradition of Sinterklaas, including gift-giving. Clement Clarke Moore wrote a poem in 1823 called "A Visit from St. Nicholas," which most of us know today as "Twas the Night Before Christmas." Moore's poem brought about the idea of Santa riding a sleigh that was pulled by reindeer and entering people's homes through the chimney to deliver gifts. A cartoonist named Thomas Nast later developed an image of Santa Claus, which over time led to the man with the white beard and red suit that we all recognize today.

New York City store owners quickly caught on to the fact that Christmas could be commercially beneficial. They all began to promote the holiday. Even back in

1830, the week before Christmas became the busiest shopping season of the year.

State Fairs and Ferris Wheels

The New York State Fair was the first state fair to ever take place. Today, it's the longest-running state fair in the United States.

The first Ferris wheel in the United States appeared at the state fair back in 1849. The Ferris wheel, which was made from iron and oak, was 50 feet high and had wooden buckets that were large enough for four adults or six children. It used ropes and was operated by hand power. It was developed by the operator of the State Fair, along with a carpenter from Scotland who had seen a similar Ferris wheel design in Edinburgh.

Soon, New York City will also be home to the second tallest Ferris wheel in the world! The New York Wheel, which is expected to be completed by 2018, will be 630-feet tall. With its location on Staten Island, the New York Wheel is expected to be one of the city's greatest landmarks. It will be one of the best places in the city to view the New York skyline, New York Harbor, and the Statue of Liberty.

Spaghetti and Meatballs

Spaghetti and meatballs are a staple in most American households. Today, people enjoy everything from zoodles (zucchini noodles) and meatballs to gluten-free spaghetti. But have you ever wondered where the original spaghetti and meatballs recipe came from? We'll give you one hint: it's not Italy.

In fact, people from Italy have been known to mock spaghetti and meatballs, recognizing the recipe as *non*-Italian! In Italy, meatballs are never served with spaghetti. The only time restaurants serve them is for American tourists.

Italy does have meatballs, but they're usually smaller than American meatballs. They're also made from different types of meats, such as turkey or fish, versus the American version of ground beef meatballs. Only certain regions of Italy, including Sicily, serve meatballs with pasta. In those instances, they're usually served with egg-based pasta or rigatoni.

So, where did spaghetti and meatballs come from? Italians who immigrated to Little Italy in New York City in the 1880s through the 1920s created the recipe. In America, food was much cheaper and the meat was more plentiful, which allowed them to eat meatballs over pasta. Spaghetti was one of the only Italian ingredients that were available in the United States at the time. They made marina sauce because canned tomatoes were easily found at local grocers.

The first recipe for spaghetti and meatballs was published in the 1920s by the National Macaroni

Manufacturers Association (now known as the National Pasta Association).

Thomas' English Muffins

Thomas' is known for its English muffins, bagels, and other bread products. Did you know the company got its start in New York City?

It all started back in 1880 when an English immigrant named Samuel Thomas opened a bakery in New York City. He created the Original "Nooks & Crannies" English muffin that so many Americans have come to enjoy today.

The secret to his English muffins was all in the cooking process. Thomas used a griddle to create an English muffin that was soft on the inside and crunchy on the outside. Although Thomas is credited for the first English muffin, his cooking method had been used in the past by other people.

It has been said that Thomas was actually trying to create a crumpet but accidentally invented the English muffin instead. Due to their name, many people believe that English muffins were popular in England before making their way to America but this isn't true.

When Samuel Thomas died in 1919, Thomas' was left to his daughter and nephews. George Weston Bakeries later went on to buy the company.

Today, Thomas' English muffins are the #1 best-selling English muffins in the United States. The company also now owns Sara Lee, Entenmann's, Stroehmann, and Arnold bread.

Red Velvet Cake

Red velvet cake, which usually consists of layers and white cream cheese frosting, has a cult-like following. Do you know how the recipe got to be so popular?

Red velvet cake got its start in 1959 at the Waldorf Astoria in New York City. It was called the "Waldorf Astoria Cake" on the hotel's menu. One guest at the hotel liked the cake so much that she asked for the recipe. Although the hotel gave it to her, she later discovered she'd been charged $100 for it. The woman was infuriated.

To get revenge on the hotel, the woman chain-mailed the recipe to hundreds of people. This helped the recipe gain popularity and sparked America's love for red velvet!

Bagels

It's often said that there's no bagel like a New York bagel.

The bagel has a long history in the Big Apple, dating back to the late 1800s when they were brought to New York by Eastern European Jewish immigrants.

Bagels were first produced in private bakeries owned

by Jewish immigrants. By 1900, there were 70 bakeries in the Lower East Side alone. The International Beigel Bakers' Union was founded in 1907 to monopolize bagel production in New York City.

Zabar's and Russ & Daughters were both opened in the early 1900s. They are two of the most iconic bagel shops that were started by Jewish immigrants.

Over time, bagel shops were no longer owned only by Jewish immigrants.

New York bagels have come a long way since they first became popular in America. For starters, the New York Bagel, as we know it today, is nearly twice the size of early bagels in the Big Apple. This change happened in the 1980s.

Today, bagels in the city also come in so many different varieties—including some that may even surprise you. You can find everything from French toast to rainbow bagels with cream cheese options that range from chocolate chip cookie dough to bacon cheddar and everything in between!

Wondering what sets New York bagels apart from other bagels? It's believed that New York City's water may have to do with why bagels in the Big Apple are so much better than everywhere else. It's believed the city's water has just the right ratio of magnesium to calcium, which makes its bagels softer and, ultimately, chewier.

Random Facts

1. The first roller coaster could be found on Coney Island. The ride was created by LaMarcus Adna Thompson in 1884. Passengers had to get off the roller coaster halfway through the ride so the car could be switched to another track.

2. Teddy bears got their start in New York City. The inspiration behind the idea of the teddy bear was President Theodore Roosevelt's refusal to shoot an injured black bear when he was hunting. Morris and Rose Michtom, who owned a candy store in Brooklyn, sewed a plush bear. They called it "Teddy's bear," after Teddy Roosevelt. The toy became such a hit that the store stopped selling candy in order to focus on teddy bears.

3. Cronuts were invented by a New York City pastry chef named Dominique Ansel. The croissant-donut hybrid first came out in May 2013 and still draws in huge crowds at the Dominque Ansel Bakery!

4. Children's museums started out in New York City! The Brooklyn Children's Museum, which opened in 1899, was the first museum in the United States that was designed for children. The Brooklyn Museum was also the first museum to offer "hands-on" exhibits.

5. Stephen Bruce, who co-founded the restaurant Serendipity 3, came up with the recipe for frozen hot chocolate. He kept his recipe a secret for 40 years before revealing it: crushed ice, 14 different types of cocoa (types unknown), and whipped cream topping.

6. The club sandwich got its start at the Saratoga Club-House in Saratoga Springs, New York.

7. The Mr. Potato Head toy was invented by George Lerner, a Brooklyn native. His invention first came about when he made plastic accessories to stick on real potatoes. Hasbro purchased the invention and released the all-plastic version of the toy in 1964. Mr. Potato Head was the first toy to ever be advertised on TV.

8. In 1898, Nikola Tesla invented the world's first remote control. Of course, the first remote didn't control a television, considering the TV wasn't invented until 1927. So, what did the first remote control operate? A boat! At the time, nobody believed the technology could even exist.

9. A chef named Charles Ranhofer at Delmonico's restaurant in Manhattan came up with the first Baked Alaska recipe in 1867. He created the cake to celebrate the United States purchasing Alaska from Russia, which is how it got its name.

10. The Reuben sandwich was created by Arnold

Reuben, who was the owner of Reuben's Deli in 1914. As the story goes, an actress who was starring in one of Charlie Chaplin's films came into the deli feeling famished. She asked Arnold to make her a combination sandwich. He threw together the few ingredients which were left on the shelves of the deli, which resulted in corned beef, Swiss cheese, and sauerkraut on rye bread with Russian dressing.

11. Sweet'n Low was founded by an entrepreneur from New York City named Benjamin Eisenstadt. He and his chemist son figured out a way to create saccharin form. Prior to Sweet'n Low, saccharin could only be manufactured in pill or liquid form. Eisenstadt named the artificial sweetener after the poem "Sweet and Low" by Alfred Tennyson.

12. Kodak was invented by a New Yorker! In 1884, George Eastman invented the roll film. Four years later, he would go on to create a push button camera. His camera was so easy to use that its motto was, "You press the button, we do the rest."

13. Tuxedos got their start in upstate New York. There was a village called Tuxedo Park, which was an exclusive resort that was founded by a guy named Pierre Lorillard IV. Lorillard, who was a tobacco tycoon wore a tailless black jacket

and black tie to a ball at the Tuxedo Club in 1886. People started to wear the fashion, which Lorillard named after the resort. The origins of the word "tuxedo" may surprise you. It came from an Algonquian word that means "round foot" or easy to surrender. It was an insult that was originally aimed at the Wolf Tribe of New York.

14. Loafers have been a timeless and popular style of shoes. Loafers originated from Syracuse, New York. The design came from James Barrett's factory, which was well-known for its handmade products.

15. Jell-O originated from New York. Peter Cooper, who was well-known for developing the first steam-powered locomotive, developed powdered gelatin. Cooper's invention was patented in 1845. Pearle Bixby Wait from LeRoy, New York got a trademark for Jell-O in 1897. He and his wife added colors and fruit flavorings to the gelatin dessert.

16. New York is to thank for one of America's most popular antibiotics. Research that was performed at Bristol Laboratories in Syracuse helped with the development of the first synthetic form of penicillin. Though they were able to develop it in 1948, the first manufactured synthetic penicillin didn't come about until 1958. The drug was mass

produced for the Armed Forces.

17. Eggs Benedict was invented in New York City. It's widely known as a hangover cure and for good reason! It was created by a hungover man who was staying at the Waldorf Astoria. The maître d was so impressed with the man's order that it was added to the hotel's menu, with a couple of changes: ham and an English muffin!

18. The fried Twinkie originated from Brooklyn! They were created by an England native named Christopher Sell. They came about because Sell tried deep-frying a lot of food items until he found something that tasted good. You can still find fried Twinkies at The Chip Chop Shop in Park Slope.

19. Scrabble was designed by an architect named Alfred Mosher Butts, who was a resident of Jackson Heights, Queens. Butts, who was a big fan of anagrams, designed the game in 1931. There's a street sign on Butt's corner in Queens, which honors the game's letter-scoring system.

20. The Tom Collins cocktail drink originated from New York City. It came about in 1874 when a guy played a prank on one of his friends at a bar in the city. He told him that a guy named Tom Collins had been in the bar talking about him. His friend went looking for the guy. The prank

continued and many people started looking for the elusive "Tom Collins." The prank, which later came to be known as the Great Tom Collins Hoax of 1874, spread to Pennsylvania and St. Louis, Missouri. Newspapers printed alleged sightings of Tom. A bartender in New York City eventually created the cocktail, which is made of gin, lemon juice, sugar, and carbonated water. Whenever anyone would come into the bar looking for the famous Tom Collins, they would unknowingly be ordering the drink.

Test Yourself – Questions and Answers

1. Which food *did not* get its start in America in New York?

    a. Hot dogs
    b. Corn dogs
    c. Pizza

2. Who started Nathan's Famous hot dogs in Coney Island?

    a. Nathan Handwerker
    b. Nathan Famous
    c. Charles Feltman

3. Which popular camera brand was started in New York by an inventor named George Eastman?

    a. Sony
    b. Canon
    c. Kodak

4. Which popular cake recipe originated from the Astoria Waldorf?

    a. Red velvet cake
    b. German chocolate cake
    c. Pineapple upside down cake

5. Which popular junk food came from New York?

    a. Corn chips
    b. Popcorn
    c. Potato chips

Answers

1. b.
2. a.
3. c.
4. a.
5. c.

CHAPTER FIVE

NEW YORK'S UNSOLVED MYSTERIES, SUPERNATURAL, AND OTHER WEIRD FACTS

Have you ever wondered what unsolved mysteries have happened in New York? Do you know what creepy folklore haunts the Empire State? Some of these facts may shock you. Some of them will give you goosebumps. Some of them are just plain weird. Read on to find out more about some of the creepiest and most bizarre things that have happened in New York.

"Amityville Horror" Took Place on Long Island

You've probably seen the movie *The Amityville Horror* or its remake. The movies and the book of the same name are based on a real-life story that took place in a house located at 112 Ocean Avenue on Long Island.

Whether you've seen the film or not, chances are there are a lot of details about the story you've never heard about.

When people think of "Amityville Horror," they mainly think of the Lutzes' version of the tale: moving into a haunted house. But before George and Kathy Lutz (and her three children) moved into the Amityville Horror house, a dark tragedy took place there.

Ronald DeFeo Jr. shot his parents, two brothers, and two sisters in the house. He murdered his family members in their beds.

Just one month after Ronald DeFeo Jr. was convicted of the killings, the Lutz family moved in.

The DeFeo's furniture was still in the house when the Lutzes moved in. They paid an additional $400 for the furniture.

The Lutz family only lived in the house for 28 days. According to an interview given by George Lutz in 2005, the family didn't know they would never return to the house. The children were frightened one night, and the Lutzes called a priest who was aware of their situation. He suggested they go somewhere for the night, but they never returned.

A few weeks after the Lutzes left the house, paranormal investigators Ed and Lorraine Warren took a photograph in the house. The picture, which has since been nicknamed the "Demonic Boy

Photograph," shows a child with glowing eyes—even though there were no kids in the house at the time of their investigation. Some believe John Matthew DeFeo's spirit is in the photo.

Although this might disappoint some people, there's a good possibility the Lutzes' experience in the Amityville Horror house may have been a hoax. William Weber, Ronald DeFeo Jr.'s lawyer, publicly stated that he and the Lutzes created the story together to "make a splash."

Even so, George and Kathy Lutz maintained that it was true until their deaths in 2006 and 2004, respectively. The children have also maintained the story over the years, though one of the sons claimed that George greatly exaggerated what went on inside the house.

If you want to get a peek at the house, know that the address has since changed at the request of the new owners. The house is now located at 108 Ocean Avenue.

Interestingly, there haven't been any reports of ghosts since the house has been under new ownership.

Nessie's Cousin May Live in Lake Champlain

It's believed that the long-lost cousin of Nessie, the Loch Ness Monster, can be found in New York's Lake Champlain. The monster, who has been nicknamed "Champ" or "Champy," has been sighted long before Nessie was ever spotted in Scotland.

The first sightings of the legendary Lake Champlain monster date back to when the Native American tribes in the area—the Iroquois and the Abenaki—spoke of seeing the creature. The Abenaki tribe called it "Tatoskok," which means "big serpent."

It has been said that the first European to report seeing Champ was Samuel de Champlain, who Lake Champlain was named after, in 1609. However, no evidence proves this to be true. It has been claimed that Samuel de Champlain described Champ as "a 20-foot serpent thick as a barrel, and a head like horse," but this quote has been found to be fake.

More than 300 sightings of Champ have been reported. To this day, people continue to report sightings.

One of the most famous sightings of the lake monster was by Sandra Massi in 1977. Massi photographed Champ, who bore a striking resemblance to Nessie in the photos.

The Fauna Communications Institute in collaboration with the *Discovery Channel* recorded noises coming from Lake Champlain resembling a beluga whale or dolphins. Beluga whales and dolphins do not live in Lake Champlain.

In 2005, a fisherman and his stepson captured video footage of Champ. Most people who have viewed the footage see the head and neck of a creature that resembles a Plesiosauria. Two former FBI forensic image analysts said the video was real and hadn't been manipulated.

The legend of Champ has drawn tourists to the Lake Champlain region. In fact, the "Champ Day" festival is celebrated in the region every July.

So, what exactly *is* Champ? Some experts believe Lake Champlain might have a breeding population of Tanystropheids, a reptile from the Middle Triassic period that resembles a long-neck dinosaur. Others believe he might be a member of the crocodile family, a Longnose Gar, a Lake Sturgeon, or even a large snapping turtle.

Whatever Champ is, it seems pretty convincing that *something* creepy is lurking in those waters.

A Neighborhood Called "The Hole" in Queens is a Body Dumping Ground

An area in the neighborhood of Ozone Park, Queens is known as "The Hole." The area spans 10 blocks between Queens and Brooklyn.

Few people actually want to live in The Hole. The land is so sunken in that it doesn't drain into the New York sewer system, making it prone to floods. The few people who live in the area keep boats in order to get from place to place during these floods.

However, the flooding isn't the only reason The Hole has hardly any residents. Ozone Park is home to John Gotti, head of the Gambino organized crime family. In 2004, one of Gotti's neighbors went missing after he accidentally hit John Gotti's son. This led to an FBI investigation, which uncovered a deep, dark secret.

The Hole was being used as a mobster burial ground. The two deceased mobsters were Philip "Philly Lucky" Giaccone and Dominick "Big Trin" Trinchera. They had been "dispatched" by John Gotti.

At the time, federal agents believed there were more bodies to be found in The Hole, but none were uncovered.

This wasn't the first time bodies had been discovered in The Hole, however. In 1981, children who were playing in The Hole found a body. That body was Mob-related, too. It had turned out to be Alphonse "Sonny Red" Indelicato, a member of the Bonanno organized crime family.

An Heiress Disappeared from Fifth Avenue and No One Ever Saw Her Again

On December 12th, 1910, a wealthy heiress and socialite named Dorothy Arnold left her family home in the Upper East Side and went out onto Fifth Avenue.

114

Dorothy, who was the daughter of a wealthy perfume importer, ran a few errands and bumped into her friend who she had a short conversation with outside a bookstore around 2 p.m. No one ever saw Dorothy again.

Her family realized she was missing a few hours later when she didn't come home for dinner. In hopes of avoiding publicity, they avoided contacting the police right away. They hired a private investigator before turning to the police after six weeks.

The police and her family tracked her last moves from the day she vanished. Marriage records were checked to see if Dorothy had eloped and fled, but there was nothing on file.

The case garnered a huge amount of publicity. Newspapers throughout the world reported on Dorothy Arnold's disappearance and followed up with leads and tips every day. Tips came in from all over the world, likely due to the family's offering of a reward of $1,000 (which is equal to about $26,000 today).

People claimed to spot Dorothy throughout both the United States and in other countries, including Italy and Chile.

According to *The Evening World*, a shop owner claimed Dorothy came into his shop in 1911 for men's clothing as a disguise. He also claimed she asked about steamer fare.

The same year, Dorothy's father received a postcard. The card read, "I am safe." While her father said it looked like her handwriting, he believed someone had copied her writing style.

One popular theory was that Dorothy had been pregnant and died during complications from an abortion. Police investigated an illegally-operated abortion clinic run out of a basement in Bellevue, Pennsylvania, which had been known as "The House of Mystery" because women disappeared after going to the clinic. One of the doctors who worked at the clinic claimed Dorothy Arnold had died there due to abortion complications. The doctor said that her body had been burned in the furnace like all of the other women who had gone missing.

Dorothy's father believed his daughter had been kidnapped and murdered.

George Griscom Jr., a guy who Dorothy had been romantically involved with, believed she had committed suicide due to her failure as an aspiring writer. She had received a rejection for a story she'd hoped to have published days before her disappearance.

After Dorothy's disappearance, George Griscom Jr. was vacationing in Italy. In early 1911, Dorothy's mother and her brother John went to Italy where

Griscom Jr. was staying to interrogate him about any information regarding her disappearance, but Griscom claimed to know nothing. Griscom then spent thousands of dollars on newspaper ads asking Dorothy to come home and claimed he wanted to marry her once she was found.

In 1916, a prisoner in Rhode Island claimed to bury a wealthy woman in a cellar at the same time of Dorothy's disappearance. The prisoner claimed he'd been hired by a man named "Little Louie," whose description matched that of George Griscom Jr. No evidence proved the prisoner's claims to be true, however.

To this day, the disappearance of Dorothy Arnold remains unsolved.

New York is Home to One of the Most Haunted Towns in the United States

Did you know one of the most haunted towns in America is located in New York? You've probably heard of the town before. It was made popular when Washington Irving wrote "The Legend of Sleepy Hollow."

Although Irving's tale was fictional, some of it is based on true legends about the town of Sleepy Hollow. One of the true parts of the tale? The legend of the infamous "Headless Horseman." During the

American Revolutionary War, a German soldier was captured and beheaded. It's long been said that a headless apparition—AKA the Headless Horseman—has been spotted throughout the grounds of Patriot Park. Another place you might spot him? The Old Dutch Church and Burial Grounds.

The Sleepy Hollow Cemetery is believed to be one of the town's most haunted places. A number of famous people are buried in the cemetery, including: Washington Irving, Andrew Carnegie, Walter Chrysler, Elizabeth Arden, and William Rockefeller. People have claimed to see apparitions in the cemetery and hear unexplained whispering.

These are just a few of the most haunted spots in Sleepy Hollow!

A Human Was Once on Display at the Bronx Zoo

One of the most bizarre moments in New York history is when the Bronx Zoo featured a human exhibit called "The Missing Link" in 1906. The exhibit featured Ota Benga, a man from the African Congo.

Benga came from a tragic background. His wife and children had been killed when there was an attack on his village. He was captured by slave traders to a man named Samuel Phillips Verner, who planned for Benga to be exhibited in the United States.

William Hornaday, the director of the Bronx Zoo, hired Ota Benga to maintain the animal habitats at first. When he realized people were more intrigued by Benga than they were in the animals, Hornaday set up an exhibit with him.

Benga took a liking to an orangutan in the zoo's Monkey House exhibit. Hornaday told him to hang his hammock there. On the first day of the exhibit, zoo visitors found Benga in the Monkey House. A sign was added to the exhibit that read, "The African Pygmy, 'Ota Benga'." The sign included Benga's height, weight, and other details.

People became outraged over the exhibit. They were infuriated by the zoo having a human on display like he was an animal. The zoo allowed Benga to roam the grounds at first before eventually removing him from zoo grounds altogether.

Verner wasn't able to find future employment for Benga. Benga was introduced to human society and later shot himself in the heart when World War I prevented him from returning to the Congo.

The American Museum of Natural History's Missing Jewels

The American Museum of Natural History was robbed on the night of October 29th, 1964. Two guys from Miami Beach broke into the JP Morgan Hall of

Gems and Minerals and stole 24 gems.

Three noteworthy gemstones were taken during the jewelry heist. They were the Star of India, the largest sapphire in the world; the Midnight Star, the blackest sapphire in existence, and the De Long Star Ruby, the world's most flawless ruby.

It's been estimated that the 24 stolen gems are worth the equivalent of $3 million today.

The robbery showed the museum's security system wasn't working properly. The burglar alarm had been dead for months. The gem room's halls' windows were also left open two inches for ventilation and there were no burglar alarms in place.

The thieves were arrested shortly after the heist.

The Star of India, the Midnight Star, and the De Long Star Ruby were all recovered and have been returned to the American Museum of Natural History, where they can still be found. Unfortunately, 14 of the 24 stolen jewels have yet to be found.

John Lennon's Ghost May Haunt an Apartment Building in New York City

John Lennon was shot dead outside his apartment building, the Dakota, in Central Park West. Years after his death, his widow Yoko Ono reported seeing his ghost sitting at the piano in the apartment they lived in together. Creepy, right? Well, it gets creepier.

John Lennon isn't the only ghost that's been known to haunt the Dakota. In fact, Lennon claimed to see an apparition himself, who he nicknamed the Crying Lady Ghost.

Other Dakota residents have reported sightings of a ghost of a girl who's estimated to be around seven years old. She smiles, laughs, and greets people when they encounter her in the hallways.

Edward Clark, the original owner of the Dakota, is said to have had a strong interest in the paranormal. He used to frequently hold séances to communicate with the dead.

There May Be Buried Treasure on Liberty Island

It has been said that Captain William Kidd buried his treasure on Liberty Island. Captain Kidd lived in New York City for four years in a house on Pearl Street, which would have allowed him to keep an eye on the island.

Captain Kidd was later hung in London in 1701 on one count of murder and five counts of piracy.

Although there may be buried treasure on Liberty Island, people have been looking for it for three centuries and turned up nothing.

There is a legend that says the treasure may be protected by ghosts, however. It has been said that a century after Captain Kidd's deaths, soldiers from Fort Wood tried to locate the treasure. They went to a psychic and followed her instructions on where to find it. When they dug in the area she'd led them to, their shovels hit a chest—and then a skull. An apparition rose from the ground with a cutlass in hand. The soldiers fled the area. When they returned, the chest was gone.

Captain Kidd was known for burying his treasures throughout the world. In 2015, an archeologist discovered buried treasure in Madagascar that is believed to have belonged to Kidd. Who knows? Maybe there *is* something on Liberty Island!

The Mystery of the Empire State Building Bermuda Triangle

You've probably heard of the Bermuda Triangle, an area in the Atlantic Ocean that is known to wreak havoc on a ship's navigation system and swallow ships. Well, the Big Apple once had a similar phenomenon a few years back.

In 2008, anytime people would drive within a five-block radius of the Empire State Building, their cars would suddenly die and not restart again. Every day, one tire and auto center in Hell's Kitchen would pick up the cars and move them a few blocks away. The cars would miraculously restart again.

It's believed that the radio signals for the broadcast beacon on the Empire State Building's tower were disabling the vehicles' alarm systems and preventing them from being able to restart. Seems like a pretty good theory, right?

Around 2013, the phenomenon suddenly stopped happening... but the broadcast beacon is still there. Strange, right? We think so, too.

The Legend of Cropsey: The Bogeyman Who Became Real

Beginning in the early 70s, there was an urban legend about "Cropsey," the bogeyman of Staten Island. Cropsey was said to be a homicidal madman.

Parents used to warn their children about Cropsey to convince them to be good. It helped them get their kids inside in time for curfew.

Even though Cropsey was an urban legend, girls in the area were going missing at the time.

There were several stories about Cropsey. In one of them, he was an escaped mental patient who was said to have a hook for a hand. He would drag children back to the abandoned ruins of Seaview Hospital, a former tuberculosis sanitarium.

Another one of the stories involved a camp located across from Willowbrook State School, a (now abandoned) mental institution on Staten Island.

Cropsey was said to be a well-respected member of the community who went mad when his son allegedly died at the camp. To get his revenge, he would scour the woods for campers to kill. Camp counselors would use the story to get campers to behave.

This urban legend turned true in 1988 when Andre Rand, a former janitor at Willowbrook State School was found guilty of kidnapping four girls. The body of one of his alleged victims, Jennifer Schweiger, was found buried behind the former mental institution. The other three girls' bodies were never found. The jury could not reach a verdict on murder charges but was able to find him guilty of kidnapping. In 2005, he was tried again for the kidnapping of another girl who went missing in 1981. Rand was again found guilty.

Police believed Rand took part in Satanism and used the children for sacrifices. It was also believed that he may have passed the children around to his homeless and mentally disabled friends who lived in Willowbrook's underground tunnel system.

Andre Rand is currently serving 25 years to life in prison. In 2037, Rand is eligible for parole.

A documentary called *Cropsey* was released in 2009 and centers on both the urban legend and Andre Rand's conviction. Two movies—*The Burning* and

Madman—were based on the urban legend of Cropsey.

A Woman Went Missing After Investigating the NYC Underground Vampire Community, Never to Be Seen Again

On July 16th, 1996, a freelance journalist named Susan Walsh disappeared from her apartment complex. She left her son with her ex-husband, who lived downstairs. Walsh was never seen again.

Early investigations centered on Walsh's ex-husband and the boyfriend she was living with. The page for July had been torn out of the calendar in her apartment, which had initially led investigators to believe that one of the men was behind her death. Although her ex-husband refused to let the police do forensic testing in their home, both he and her boyfriend were ruled out as suspects.

Another theory was that she was being stalked. Days before her disappearance, Walsh had been recorded in a group interview for a documentary her friend was working on, called *Stripped*. The documentary was about women working in the sex industry, and Walsh was a former exotic dancer. In the recording, she had mentioned having a "stalker."

Walsh didn't tell anyone who she thought the stalker was, but 10 years later, the *New York Post* published an article stating that Walsh's boyfriend at the time of her disappearance claimed another one of her ex-boyfriends had been stalking her.

Many believe Susan Walsh's investigative journalism may have had to do with her disappearance. Walsh had written an article for *The Village Voice* in which she claimed the Russian Mafia owned a strip club chain and were forcing young girls into the sex industry. Some believed the Russian Mafia was responsible for her disappearance.

But the most intriguing theory of all links her disappearance to the New York City underground vampire community. During the weeks leading up to her disappearance, Walsh had been working on an article about the vampire community in Manhattan. The article ultimately ended up being rejected.

Is it possible that Susan Walsh got too close to the vampire cult? Some have even wondered if she might have joined them, though her family claimed she would have never left her son or without letting anyone know where she was going.

An author and vampire expert named Katherine Ramsland went undercover in the underground vampire community to try to find out what may have happened to Walsh. She later wrote a book about it called *Piercing the Darkness: Undercover with Vampires in America Today*.

Ramsland claimed that the underground vampire community in Manhattan was ultimately harmless. They took part in consensual blood sharing, blood consumption, and other unique fetishes, but Ramsland doesn't believe the vampire community had anything to do with Walsh's disappearance.

Ramsland does note that the vampire community does gain benefits from the public viewing them as a threat. Several people from the vampire community had committed crimes. Could Susan Walsh have just met the wrong person from the cult at the wrong time?

Walsh's disappearance was featured on *Unsolved Mysteries*. Her disappearance remains an unsolved mystery to this day.

The Legend of the Hudson River Ghost Ship

Well, here's a different kind of urban legend for you. Forget about Bigfoot, vampires or UFOs. Ever hear of the Hudson River Ghost Ship? It's also been called the Hudson Valley Ghost Ship or the Brooklyn Ghost Ship. Whatever you want to call it, the legend is pretty creepy.

Ever since New York was known as New Amsterdam, there have been reports of a mysterious ghost ship floating down the Hudson River.

It has been said the ship appears without a flag and

in the form of an apparition. Many believe the ship is the ghost of the Half Moon, Henry Hudson's ship which was destroyed in 1618. Others have theorized that the ship may be the ghost of an old prison ship. Whatever the case, sightings are reported to this day.

One man who reported seeing the Hudson River Ghost Ship says it's a wooden ship with three empty masts. The eeriest part about his description was that the ship was silent until it was about 50 feet away from him.

Over the years, the ship has come to be known as the "The Storm Ship." The ship is said to appear just prior to a storm sets in. Some sailors believe seeing the ship means bad weather is coming and take it as a sign to stay off the waters. Some even believe the ship appears before someone dies.

We're pretty sure that if we saw the ghost ship, we'd be nowhere near the water!

The Wall Street Bombing Mystery

Did you know there was a terror attack in New York City that happened long before the September 11th attacks? Coincidentally, this attack happened during the month of September, too.

On September 20th, 1920, a bomb exploded from a horse-drawn wagon in front of 23 Wall Street. The wagon had been loaded with 500 pounds of small iron weights and dynamites.

Thirty-eight people and one horse were killed from the attack, with hundreds more being injured from the shrapnel and glass that fell out of building windows.

No one took credit for the bombing. At the time, many people believed the communists were responsible for the attack, but no person or group ever claimed responsibilityfor the terrorist attack.

The city was anxious to reopen Wall Street the following day, which resulted in important evidence being destroyed. An investigation that lasted three years turned up nothing.

In 1944, the FBI said they believed Italian anarchists were responsible for the bombing, but even this theory has never really been proven.

We may never know who was responsible for the Wall Street bombing.

The Hotel Chelsea is Believed to be Haunted

The Hotel Chelsea in Manhattan is said to be one of the most haunted spots in New York City. The hotel, which has had a number of celebrity guests, tends to attract a lot of people who are on the hunt for ghosts.

The fact that the Chelsea might be haunted isn't all that surprising, considering it's dark and tragic past.

Sid Vicious from the Sex Pistols is believed to have stabbed his girlfriend, Nancy Spungen, at the Chelsea in 1978. He was arrested and set to stand trial for her murder, but he overdosed on heroin in 1979. People have reported seeing and hearing Sid Vicious and Nancy Spungen around the hotel floors.

Elevators are said to mysteriously stop at random floors. Legend has it that it's the ghost of Sid getting on the elevator because he's too lazy to take the stairs.

Famous poet Dylan Thomas also died at the Chelsea in 1953. His death was caused by pneumonia. Guests have reported seeing Thomas's face near Room 206, the room he died in.

Other people have reported hearing high-pitched screams and footsteps throughout the hotel. In 2009, three women captured skeletons in a photo in the closet, even though there wasn't actually a skeleton in the room. They claimed the lights in their room kept flickering on and off, the sink kept turning on and off, and there were strange bubbles that rose from the drain.

Don't believe it? The only way to find out is to spend a night at the hotel yourself!

Random Facts

1. There was one unsolved homicide in New York City on the day of the September 11th attacks. Henry Siwiak, a Polish immigrant, was shot in Brooklyn. He has been named "the last person killed in New York on 9/11," but his death wasn't relevant to the attacks. It's believed that the circumstances behind his murder may have been solved if so much police attention hadn't been diverted to the 9/11 attacks. It has been theorized that his killer might have believed he was responsible for the attacks since he was wearing camouflage at the time of his death and spoke poor English.

2. There was a riot in New York City in 1922 over straw hats. Yes, you read that right. People fought. Over straw hats. Why? Well, it was believed that straw hats were only appropriate summer attire. Wearing them in autumn was considered not only inappropriate, many considered it to be offensive. Similar riots broke out through all of the Northeast, but the original riot started in thee Big Apple. The riot, which lasted for three days, happened when straw hat hating men terrorized the streets of New York. They snatched and destroyed straw hats, and young men got into fights. Thankfully, no one

died during the riot, but there were several injuries.

3. A common fear among New Yorkers is alligators in the sewage system. These fears aren't entirely baseless—there have been 12 sightings of alligators in New York City sewers over the years. People began to panic about coming face-to-face with an alligator in the Big Apple when the *New York Times* published an article titled "Alligator Found in Uptown Sewer" in 1935. It's believed the alligators found in the city were exotic pets that escaped down sewer grates and open manholes, but it's a widespread legend that people were flushing baby alligators down toilets.

4. There have been numerous reports of sightings of UFOs in New York over the years. In 2017 alone, there were 169 sightings across the entire state with 23% of those sightings hailing from the Big Apple. There were 39 sightings across New York City that year, according to the National UFO Reporting Center. Of those sightings, 10 were reported in Queens, nine were reported in Manhattan, three were reported in the Bronx, and two were reported on Staten Island. This is a switch from 2016 where the most UFO sightings were reported in Manhattan.

5. There's an urban legend known as Central Park's

Skating Sisters. People have reported seeing apparitions at Wollman Rink in Central Park. It's believed they're the spirits of the Van der Voort sisters, Janet and Rosetta. Their overprotective father rarely allowed them to leave the family home without being accompanied, except for when they went ice skating. The sisters grew into lonely spinsters who died months apart in 1880. Since then, their ghosts have been spotted. The sisters are said to wear red and purple dresses with a bustle, and their feet don't touch the ground. It's also been said that they appear more when overprotective parents are around.

6. Richard Colvin Cox is the only cadet to have ever disappeared from the military academy in West Point, New York. He allegedly told his friends he was going to have dinner with a friend named George. Cox was never seen again. Police received an anonymous tip that a murderer named Robert Frisbee was linked to Cox's disappearance. Although Frisbee was in West Point at the time and matched George's description, no evidence linked him to Richard Colvin Cox.

7. A postal carrier named Joseph Brucato was caught hoarding 40,000 pieces of undelivered mail in the firetrap of his apartment. Brucato had been hoarding the mail for a decade. It included

bills, birthday cards, junk mail, coupon booklets, and anything else you can imagine. Brucato blamed his depression and alcoholism for his sticky fingers.

8. A widespread myth is that New York City is home to 8 million rats. If you suffer from a rat phobia, try not to worry *too* much when you're in the Big Apple. The Department of Health claims that there are really only 2 million rats in the city.

9. There have been numerous sightings of Big Foot and his tracks in Upstate New York. If he's out there, New Yorkers seem to be welcoming of him. There's a local ordinance to protect Sasquatch in Whitehall, New York, and two festivals in the area (The Sasquatch Calling Festival and the Chautauqua Lake Bigfoot Expo) celebrate the legendary creature.

10. Mountain lions no doubt exist in the wild, but it's been said that the cougar is extinct in the Northeastern region of the United States. People often report mountain lion sightings in Upstate New York. It's even been rumored that the Department of Environmental Conservation releases mountain lions into the wild to keep the deer population under control. The DEC denies these claims and says that any isolated sightings in New York have been mountain lions that were previously being held captive or one incident in

which a cougar traveled 1,800 miles from South Dakota to New York state.

11. Arnold Rothstein was murdered in New York City in 1928. Rothstein was a kingpin of the Jewish mob who was well-known for gambling and racketeering. Rothstein was most famous for fixing the World Series in 1919. He allegedly paid the players of the Chicago White Sox to deliberately lose the World Series so that he would win $350,000. Rothstein was never charged with the crime, however. In 1928, Rothstein was shot in the stomach when he walked into a room at the Park Central Hotel for a poker game. Although Rothstein survived for a few days, he never told anyone who had shot him—though it was suspected that he was assassinated by someone who he owed money, as he owed more than $500,000 in gambling debts.

12. An urban legend says there was once a time traveler in Times Square. In 1950, a man dressed in clothing from the Victorian era randomly appeared in the middle of the intersection. He is said to have appeared confused and disoriented. The man was hit and killed by a taxi. At the morgue, it was discovered that the man had letters and banknotes in his pocket with the year 1876 written on them. The paper didn't appear worn or aged.

13. In Rochester, New York, there's a legend about a lady in white. As the tale goes, the woman's teenage daughter went missing after a walk one day. The woman spent every day walking along the shores of Lake Ontario in search of her daughter before eventually jumping off the cliff and into the lake to commit suicide. Today, teenagers who go to the lake claim to see her ghost.

14. Today, violent crime rates are the lowest they've ever been in New York City. In 2017, there were only 290 homicides in the Big Apple. This is the lowest number since the 1940s. In the 1980s and early 1990s, violent crime rates spiked due to a crack epidemic in New York City.

15. The Landmark Theater in Syracuse, New York is believed to be haunted by the ghost of a woman who died when she fell off a balcony.

16. In 2003, people were frightened to learn a tiger was being kept in an apartment in Harlem. Antoine Yates got the tiger, which he called Ming, when it was just a cub. The cub eventually grew into a 500-pound tiger who ate buckets of chicken every day. Yates got Ming a companion: a 7-foot alligator named Al. Yates was caught with the tiger after it attacked a rescued house cat. The veterinary hospital let authorities know the cat's wounds were suspicious.

17. Yates wasn't the first to keep a wildcat in the city. Back in the 1950s, a gangster named Crazy Joe Gallo kept a lion in the basement of a club owned by Mondo, a "midget mascot" for the Mafia. Joe Gallo used to try to intimidate people by taking the lion for walks through the neighborhood.

18. Three men pretended to be cops at a GameStop on Staten Island so they could skip the lines to get their copies of *Grand Theft Auto V*. They were later pulled over and charged with criminal impersonation.

19. A seventeen-year-old in Bushwick, Brooklyn was charged with terrorism after he posted an emoji of a police officer in between two emojis of guns on his Facebook wall. The NYPD claimed the "terroristic" emoji threats made them fear for their safety and public safety.

20. The Rolling Hills Asylum in East Bethany, New York is believed to be haunted. Patients who have died at the mental institution are believed to haunt the floors.

Test Yourself – Questions and Answers

1. Who is the first European who allegedly saw the Lake Champlain monster?

   a. Henry Hudson
   b. Samuel de Champlain
   c. Dylan Thomas

2. Captain William Kidd's buried treasure might be found where?

   a. "The Hole"
   b. Staten Island
   c. Liberty Island

3. There's been panic about which of the following animals being found in New York City's sewers?

   a. Alligators
   b. Snakes
   c. Tigers

4. Which famous person died at the Chelsea Hotel?

   a. Dylan Thomas
   b. Sid Vicious
   c. Arnold Rothstein

5. The legendary Staten Island bogeyman was named:

   a. "Little Louie"
   b. Cropsey
   c. Bogey

Answers

1. b.
2. c.
3. a.
4. a.
5. b.

CHAPTER SIX

NEW YORK SPORTS: BASEBALL, FOOTBALL, AND MORE!

You probably know New York is home to the most popular baseball team in the United States, but do you know the legend behind why their uniforms have pinstripes? Do you know which international sporting event has been held in New York twice? Do you know which athletes are from the Empire State? Here, you'll find the answers to all of these questions, along with other New York sports facts!

Mike Tyson's Career Started Out at a Juvenile Detention Center in New York

Mike Tyson, former heavyweight champion, is considered to be a legend. Did you know his career was started in New York?

Mike Tyson was born in Brownsville, Brooklyn in 1966. Tyson grew up in and around neighborhoods with crime rates. He often got into fights with kids who made fun of his lips and high-pitched voice. By the time he was 13, Tyson had been arrested nearly 40 times.

Tyson ended up in the Tyron School for Boys, a juvenile detention center in Johnstown, New York. It was there that Tyson began to box. His talent was discovered by a former boxer named Bobby Stewart.

Stewart took Tyson under his wing and trained him. Stewart later introduced Tyson to trainer and boxing manager Cus D'Amato. D'Amato ran a gym in the Catskills. When Mike Tyson's mom died when he was just 16 years old, D'Amato became his legal guardian.

Mike made his first boxing debut when he was 18 in Albany, New York. Tyson defeated his opponent, Hector Mercedes, in a knock-out during the first round. Tyson went onto win all but two of his first 28 fights before winning his first heavyweight championship in 1986.

After he was convicted of rape in 1992, people believed Tyson's career was over but it wasn't. In 1996, he went out to win the WBC and WBA titles.

In 2011, Mike Tyson was inducted into the Boxing Hall of Fame.

New York Has Hosted the Winter Olympics

Twice

The Winter Olympics have been held in Lake Placid, New York twice.

The 3rd Winter Olympics were held in Lake Placid back in 1932. The games were opened by Franklin D. Roosevelt, who was the Governor of New York at the time.

Some of the highlights from the 1932 Winter Olympics include:

- Eddie Eagan became the first and only Olympian who won gold medals in both the winter and summer Olympics. At the 1920 Summer Olympics, he won a gold medal in boxing. In 1932, he won the gold in bobsleigh.

- Three-time winning Olympic champion Sonja Henie won her second gold medal in figure skating.

- The United States won a total of 12 Olympic medals, half of which were gold medals.

In 1980, the 13th Winter Olympics were also held in Lake Placid. Highlights from that year include:

- Artificial snow was used in the Olympics for the very first time.

- The USA's men's hockey team won the gold medal, defeating the Soviet team 4-3. The team wasn't projected to win. Their achievement became internationally known as the "Miracle on Ice."

- Eric Heiden won four gold medals and set one world record in speed skating. He became the first Olympics champion to win all five of the speed skating events and the first of three to ever win five gold medals at the same Games. To date, Heiden still holds the record of being the only Olympics champion to win five gold medals at a single Winter Games.

- The People's Republic of China entered the Olympics for the first time.

- The games were opened by United States Vice President Walter Mondale, marking the last time the Olympics were opened by an American Vice President.

And There's a Lake Placid Olympic Museum!

You can visit the Lake Placid Olympic Museum, which honors the 1932 and 1980 Winter Olympic Games.

A number of artifacts can be found at the museum. Some of these include Olympic torches, antique ice skates, bobsled equipment, Olympic uniforms, medals, official Olympics posters, and more. You'll also find artifacts relating to the champions of the

Olympics games from 1932 and 1980.

The museum also commemorates Charles Jewtraw, an Olympics gold medalist from the Lake Placid region. Jewtraw was the first speed skater to win a gold medal at the 1st Winter Olympics in 1924.

You can also visit the Olympic Center, which has been named the Herb Brooks Arena. This is where the "Miracle on Ice" took place!

The New York Yankees Weren't Always Called the Yankees

It's hard to imagine the New York Yankees being called anything other than the Yankees today, but did you know the team was once named something else first?

In 1901, the New York Yankees were founded in Baltimore, Maryland. John McGraw owned the team, which was known as the Baltimore Orioles. The American League voted to move the team to New York.

When the Baltimore Orioles moved to New York in 1903, their name was changed to the New York Highlanders. Their first stadium was at Hilltop Park in Manhattan.

Even though they were called the Highlanders, a lot of sportswriters began to refer to them as the "Yanks" or "Yankees" because they were in the American

League.

In 1913, the team was renamed the Yankees. At this time, they moved to the Polo Grounds stadium, which they shared with the New York Giants.

The New York Yankees' Pinstripe Uniforms May Have Been Designed for Babe Ruth

While this is technically an urban legend, it seems to be commonly accepted as the truth. It's been said that Babe Ruth, who is undeniably the most famous baseball player of all-time, is the reason the New York Yankees have their pinstripe uniforms.

Babe Ruth was a pretty large guy, at least as far as baseball players go. Rumor has it that the team chose to go with pinstripe uniforms to help make Babe Ruth look thinner than he really was.

Some argue that this can't be true. The team initially adopted their pinstripe uniforms in 1912, back when they were still called the Highlanders. Babe Ruth didn't join the team until years later. Could it all be a total coincidence? We're not really sure, but the theory seems to be commonly accepted by most Yankees fanatics.

The New York Yankees and the New York

Giants Were the First Teams to Retire Players' Numbers

When a baseball number is retired in the MLB or the NFL, it's to ensure no future players will wear them. People will only ever associate the number with that particular player.

Lou Gehrig was the first player in MLB history to have his number, 4, retired by the New York Yankees.

Today, Lou Gehrig is best-known for his disease, amyotrophic lateral sclerosis. That disease is now named after him and referred to simply as "Lou Gehrig's Disease."

The disease is what forced the former New York Yankees player into voluntary retirement on July 4th, 1939. The disease had begun to affect his performance. Gehrig died just two years later at the young age of 37.

Gehrig played for the Yankees from 1923 to 1939. During that time, he set a couple of records. He had the highest number of grand slams, which was later broken by Alex Rodriguez. He also held the record for the most consecutive games played at 2,130. That record wouldn't be broken for another 56 years when it was surpassed by Carl Ripken, Jr.

The second player in MLB history whose number

was retired was Babe Ruth.

The New York Giants were also the first football team in the history of the NFL to retire a player's number. In 1935, Ray Flaherty left the team to become the head coach for the Redskins. His jersey number was the No. 1.

Babe Ruth Was Sold to the New York Yankees to Finance a Broadway Production

Today, he may be recognized as the New York Yankees' greatest legend, but unlike Lou Gehrig, Babe Ruth's careers didn't start and end with the Yankees.

Before he became a Yankees player, Ruth played for the Boston Red Sox first. In 1919, the New York Yankees bought him for more than $125,000, which is estimated to be about $1.45 million today.

Harry Frazee, owner of the Red Sox at the time, was also a theatrical agent, producer, and director. Rumor has it that the money Frazee sold Ruth to the Yankees for went to support the Broadway musical *No, No, Nanette.*

Although Babe Ruth was hesitant about leaving the Sox, he agreed to an initial two-year contract at $10,000 a year.

A lot of Red Sox fans blamed Frazee for selling Babe Ruth to the Yankees. His decision has been called

"The Curse of the Bambino." Fans blamed the move for the lack of championships the Boston Red Sox accrued from 1918. The dry spell finally ended in 2004 when the team finally won against the St. Louis Cardinals in the October Classic.

A New York Baseball Team Has Played Some of the Longest Games in MLB History

Did you know that a New York baseball team has played not just one but *three* of the longest games in Major League Baseball history? And—surprise—it's not the New York Yankees!

The longest game played by the New York Mets was against the Atlanta Braves. The game lasted a total of eight hours, fifteen minutes. This includes rain delays.

When the game finally ended at 3:55 a.m., the Mets won 16-13.

New York is Home to the Baseball Hall of Fame

The National Baseball Hall of Fame and Museum is located in Cooperstown, New York.

The Hall of Fame was founded by Stephen Carlton Clark in 1939. Clark, who owned a local hotel, had hoped to draw tourists to Coopersburg, which had taken an economic hit during the Great Depression. Today, the Hall of Fame is considered the most significant establishment for the study of baseball in the United States.

So, what exactly can you expect to see at the museum? The exhibits contain thousands of MLB-related artifacts. You'll see pictures, watch video footage, and listen to audio that will help you learn more about the game.

Some of the many exhibits you'll find at the Baseball Hall of Fame and Museum include: Babe Ruth: His Life and Legend, Diamond Dreams: Women in Baseball, Pride and Passion: The African American Baseball Experience, Baseball at the Movies, Taking the Field: The 19th Century, and Today's Game.

You'll also want to check out the Hall of Fame Plaque Gallery, which is home to the bronze plaques to more than 300 players who have been inducted into the Hall of Fame.

The Super Bowl Has Been Won by New York Teams a Total of Five Times

Did you know the Super Bowl has been won by New York NFL teams five times? The New York Giants have won the Super Bowl four times, while the New York Jets have won it once.

The Giants won the Super Bowl during the following years:

1. 1987: The Giants defeated the Broncos by 39-20.

2. 1991: The Giants won against the Buffalo Bills with a score of 20-19.

3. 2008: The Giants beat the New England Patriots, winning 17-14.

4. 2012: The Giants defeated the New England Patriots by 21-17.

The Giants are tied with the Packers for the team with the 3rd highest number of Super Bowl titles.

The Jets won the Super Bowl in 1968. They defeated the Baltimore Colts with a score of 16-7.

The New York Rangers Are One of the Oldest Hockey Teams in the NHL

Did you know the New York Rangers were one of the first National Hockey League teams to be formed? The team was formed in 1926. It was one of the "Original Six"—the first six teams that entered the NHL. The other teams from the Original Six include: the Chicago Blackhawks, the Boston Bruins, the Detroit Red Wings, the Montreal Canadiens, and the Toronto Maple Leafs.

The New York Rangers began breaking records their very first season in the NHL. Their first season, they finished with the highest record in the league. Rangers player Bill Cook was also the highest scorer that season.

In 1928, the Rangers won their first Stanley Cup. They were the first—and remain the only—team to win the Stanley Cup within two years of joining the league.

In the first six years, the Rangers went to the finals four times.

Both Hockey and Basketball Games Are Played at Madison Square Garden

Did you know that both hockey games *and* basketball games are played at Madison Square Garden?

The MSG arena is home to both the NBA's New York Knicks and the NHL's New York Rangers. In fact, games from both teams have been played in the arena on the very same day. Wondering how that can even be possible?

During hockey season, the ice can be found underneath the stage that's used for the basketball court. It's kept frozen with insulated material.

While the New York Knicks play their home games at Madison Square Garden, they haven't always had the greatest luck there. Their second worst loss in team history happened at MSG when they lost by a 50 points loss to the Dallas Mavericks.

The New York Rangers' retired numbers can be found hanging from the rafters of the MSG arena. One of those numbers belonged to the most well-known Rangers player, Wayne Gretzky.

Nina Kuscsik is a Brooklyn Native

Nina Kuscsik, a native of Brooklyn, is famous for setting several historical records for female long-distance runners.

In 1970, she became the first female to run the New York City marathon. Kuscsik won the races two years in a row in 1972 and 1973. In 1972, she was also the first woman to win the Boston Marathon.

At the time, the prizes for winning the marathon for women were wreaths and a bowl of stew. Today, female marathon champions are now able to earn six-figure rewards—a feat that Kuscsik is often credited for.

Twelve-Time Olympic Medallist Ryan Lochte is From New York

Twelve-time Olympic medalist Ryan Lochte is a household name. He ranks second in men's swimming, just behind Michael Phelps. Did you know he's a New York native?

Ryan Lochte was born in Rochester, New York. He grew up in Bristol, New York and attended Bloomfield Central Schools until his family moved to Florida when Ryan was 12 years old.

Lochte first began to learn to swim when he was living in New York. His father was a swim instructor and often kicked Ryan out of his swim classes for misbehaving. It wasn't until junior high school that Ryan really got serious about learning to swim. He began to train harder after he lost at the Junior Olympics.

Ryan Lochte went on to six gold, three silver, and three bronze Olympic medals. Lochte holds the world record for short course 400-meter individual medley and both the long and short course 200-meter individual medley.

In 2016, Lochte sparked a lot of controversies when he lied about being robbed in Rio de Janeiro, Brazil during the Summer Olympics. Later accounts of the incident were different from the first version, which made people question the validity of the story. Lochte was put on probation from swimming for 10 months.

Baseball Might Become the State's Official Sport, But Not Every New Yorker Would Agree with That Decision

There have been talks about making baseball New York's official state sport. In a lot of ways, the decision makes sense.

New York is home to the Yankees, the most popular (and arguably the most successful) team in the MLB. Many of the greatest MLB players of all-time played for the Yankees, such as: Babe Ruth, Lou Gehrig, Joe DiMaggio, Yogi Berra, Derek Jeter, Mariano Rivera, and Alex Rodriguez—just to name a few of the *many*.

New York City is also one of only four metropolitan cities that's home to more than one baseball team.

There are also two minor league baseball teams in New York City.

The Baseball Hall of Fame is also located in New York and for good reason. New York City is rich with both baseball history and notorious legends.

But despite all that, football is the most followed sport in New York City! Many have argued that football should be the official state sport... if one is ever chosen at all.

Random Facts

1. NBA legend Michael Jordan was born in Brooklyn, New York, but his family moved to Wilmington when he was a toddler. Jordan later went on to defeat the New York Knicks when he played for the Chicago Bulls.

2. A number of records were set by the New York Yankees. The Yankees have won the most consecutive World Series titles—and they've done it more than once. They won between the years of 1996 and 2000 and then again between 1927 and 1932 and 1937 and 1941. Mariano Rivera has pitched the most World Series games. The only MLB players to ever hit three home runs in a World Series were Babe Ruth and Reggie Jackson. Derek Jeter is the only MLB player to be named both the All-Star MVP and the World Series MVP in the same year (2000). Orlando Hernandez has the highest strikeout rate of any MLB player who has pitched in the World Series. Yogi Berra held the record for playing more World Series games than any other Yankees player.

3. Although the New York Giants are considered a New York football team, they're based out of New Jersey. Their home stadium is MetLife Stadium in East Rutherford, New Jersey. When

the team was founded in 1925, however, they played at Polo Grounds in Manhattan and later spent two decades playing at Yankees stadium. Currently, the only NFL team that actually plays in the Empire State are the Buffalo Bills.

4. The Buffalo Bills are the only New York NFL team who hasn't won a Super Bowl championship. They also are the only team in the NFL who has lost four Super Bowl games in a row in the years of 1990, 1991, 1992, and 1993. Their losses became a joke and the team lost a lot of fans due to their consecutive losses. At one point, it was even said that "bills" stood for "Boy, I love losing Super (Bowls)."

5. In 1927, the New York Yankees had a lineup known as "Murderers Row." It included: Babe Ruth, Lou Gehrig, Bob Meusel, Earle Combs, Mark Koenig, and Tony Lazzeri. These first six batters were carefully chosen to intimidate the opposing pitcher. Between the years of 1923 and 1962, they won 20 World Series titles with their all-star lineup.

6. The New York Yankees have the highest number of World Series titles of any team in the MLB. As of 2009, they've won a total of 27 World Series titles. The team with the second highest number of World Series titles is the St. Louis Cardinals, who only have 11 titles.

7. Nancy Lieberman was born in Brooklyn and was raised in Far Rockaway, New York. She has been considered one of the best women's basketball players of all-time. Lieberman was nicknamed "Lady Magic," which was a nod at "Magic" Johnson. Lieberman has been inducted into both the Basketball Hall of Fame and the Women's Basketball Hall of Fame.

8. The New York Jets were originally called the Titans of New York when they were established back in 1959. Like the Giants and Yankees, they first began playing at Polo Ground in Manhattan. When the team went under new ownership in 1963, they were renamed the Jets and were moved to Shea Stadium.

9. The New York Giants were the first football team in the NFL to retire a player's number.

10. As of 2012, the New York Giants had never lost an NFC Championship Game.

11. The New York Mets' full legal team name is the New York Metropolitan Baseball Club, Inc. At one point, owner Joan Whitney Payson considered naming the team the Bees, the Continentals, the Avengers, the Meadowlarks, or the Islanders.

12. The New York Giants' full legal team name is "The New York Giants Football Team." The

word "Football" was added to the name in 1937 because they wanted to differentiate themselves from the former New York Giants baseball team, who later moved to San Francisco.

13. Former New York Yankees manager Joe Torre was born in Brooklyn, New York. Under his management, the Yankees won four World Series titles. Prior to managing the Yankees, Torre played for the Milwaukee/Atlanta Braves, St. Louis Cardinals, and New York Mets. Torre holds the world record of scoring 2,000 hits as a baseball player and 2,000 wins as a baseball manager. As of 2018, Joe Torre was the chief baseball officer for the MLB.

14. The New York Knicks' legal franchise name is the New York Knickerbockers. Ned Irish, the owner of the team, wanted the name to be distinctive of New York. "Knickerbocker" originated from Washington Irving's pen name Diedrich Knickerbocker, under which he wrote a satirical history book called *A History of New-York from the Beginning of the World to the End of the Dutch Dynasty*. The name "Knickerbocker" had been used to describe Dutch settlers in New Amsterdam and later all New Yorkers. Irish had his staff members vote on the name of his basketball team and the New York Knickerbockers got the highest number of votes.

15. The Mets have a number of regional landmarks in its logo, such as Woolworth Building, the Empire State Building, and the United Nations Building. The bridge in the logo is meant to represent all five boroughs.

16. Country musician Garth Brooks tried out for the New York Mets in 2000. After a sad 0-17 at bat, the Mets opted not to add them to their rotation. At the time, it was believed to be a big publicity stunt. However, Brooks later went on to try out for the Kansas City Royals in 2004. It was there that he got his only hit. We think he should probably stick to country music.

17. The New York Mets are the first MLB team to trade a player back to his original team. Harry Chiti was originally traded from the Cleveland Indians to the New York Mets with the agreement that the Mets would trade a player back to the Indians later on. When the time came, they gave Chiti back to Cleveland.

18. Vince Lombardi, the head coach of the Green Bay Packers in the 1960s, was born in Brooklyn.

19. The Knicks made a trade for Brooklyn native Carmelo Anthony. In the beginning, people didn't think the trade was worth it. Since then, Anthony has proven to be one of the Knicks' best players and made it to the Hall of Fame.

20. In 2000, Woody Johnson paid $635 million for the New York Jets. Johnson outbid Charles Dolan, whose company Cablevision owns Madison Square Garden, the New York Rangers, and the New York Knicks.

Test Yourself – Questions and Answers

1. The Winter Olympics have been hosted twice in which of the following New York towns?

   a. Lake Champlain
   b. Lake Placid
   c. Rochester

2. According to urban legend, why do the New York Yankees uniforms have pinstripes?

   a. Because it was Babe Ruth's favorite pattern
   b. Babe Ruth thought pinstripes would bring good luck to the team
   c. Pinstripes would slim Babe Ruth's larger figure

3. Which famous sports legend was *not* born in New York?

   a. Babe Ruth
   b. Michael Jordan
   c. Mike Tyson

4. Which Hall of Fame can be found in Cooperstown, New York?

   a. The Basketball Hall of Fame
   b. The Baseball Hall of Fame
   c. The Football Hall of Fame

5. Which country musician tried out for the New York Mets?

   a. Blake Shelton

   b. Keith Urban

   c. Garth Brooks

Answers

1. b.

2. c.

3. a.

4. b.

5. c.

DON'T FORGET YOUR FREE BOOKS

GET THEM FOR FREE ON
WWW.TRIVIABILL.COM

OTHER BOOKS IN THIS SERIES

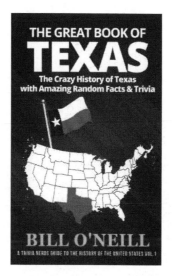

Are you looking to learn more about Texas? Sure, you've heard about the Alamo and JFK's assassination in history class, but there's so much about the Lone Star State that even natives don't know about. In this trivia book, you'll journey through Texas's history, pop culture, sports, folklore, and so much more!

In The Great Book of Texas, some of the things you will learn include:

Which Texas hero isn't even from Texas?

Why is Texas called the Lone Star State?

Which hotel in Austin is one of the most haunted hotels in the United States?

Where was Bonnie and Clyde's hideout located?

Which Tejano musician is buried in Corpus Christi?

What unsolved mysteries happened in the state?

Which Texas-born celebrity was voted "Most Handsome" in high school?

Which popular TV show star just opened a brewery in Austin?

You'll find out the answers to these questions and many other facts. Some of them will be fun, some of them will creepy, and some of them will be sad, but all of them will be fascinating! This book is jampacked with everything you could have ever wondered about Texas.

Whether you consider yourself a Texas pro or you know absolutely nothing about the state, you'll learn something new as you discover more about the state's past, present, and future. Find out about things that weren't mentioned in your history book. In fact, you might even be able to impress your history teacher with your newfound knowledge once you've finished reading! So, what are you waiting for? Dive in now to learn all there is to know about the Lone Star State!

MORE BOOKS BY BILL O'NEILL

I hope you enjoyed this book and learned something new. Please feel free to check out some of my previous books.